Unsparing of herself as "informant,
and a delight to read, Amal Ghandou
circumstances of a small but very inf
Stylish, witty, and heartbreaking, this
contribution to our current soul-search

—**Ahdaf Soueif,**
Novelist, essayist, and activist

Amal Ghandour has written a nostalgic book with glimmers of brilliant
personal, social and political observations and probing about Jordan
and Lebanon, about wars and longings, about a rich life of upheavals
and laments.

—**Raja Shehadeh,**
Palestinian writer and lawyer, and founder of the human rights
organization Al-Haq

This Arab Life *is a sweeping retrospective on a generation's historic*
complicity in the present travails plaguing the Arab world. The book is,
at once, intimate, far-reaching, political, angry, melancholic, funny, and
nostalgic. Ghandour's reflections on her life, and on the decisions taken
by her and her peers as they came of age in the eighties and nineties,
offers important insight for anyone seeking to understand how we got
to where we are today in the region. The book is a cautionary tale of
political acquiescence, and one that is, like many Arabs, stuck between
an urgent impulse to act, to change, to hope, alongside an overwhelming
sense of despair and apathy.

—**Tarek Baconi,**
Author of **Hamas Contained: The Rise and Pacification of**
Palestinian Resistance *and president of the board of al-Shabaka:*
The Palestinian Policy Network

Also by Amal Ghandour

About This Man Called Ali

This Arab Life

This Arab Life

A Generation's Journey into Silence

Amal Ghandour

**BOLD
STORY
PRESS**

Washington, DC

Bold Story Press, Washington, DC 20016
www.boldstorypress.com

Copyright © 2022 by Amal Ghandour

All rights reserved. No part of this book may be reproduced or used in any manner without written permission of the copyright owner except for the use of quotations in a book review. Requests for permission or further information should be submitted through info@boldstorypress.com.

This book is a memoir and it reflects the author's present recollections of experiences over time.

First edition published October 2022

Library of Congress Control Number: 2022904268

ISBN: 978-1-954805-32-3 (hardback)
ISBN: 978-1-954805-26-2 (paperback)
ISBN: 978-1-954805-27-9 (e-book)

Text design by Laurie Entringer
Cover design by Laurie Entringer
Author photo by Cherine Jokhdar

Page 72: Text used with permission. © 2022 Nizar Qabbani Publications. All Rights Reserved.

Printed in the United States of America
10 9 8 7 6 5 4 3 2 1

For my father and mother,

Ali and Altaf

I have for my country the affection of the disenchanted. A love that is secret and strong. A passion. I love the people and the skies, which I try to decipher in books and in glimpses at night. I dream of power, of sovereignty for my people, of consciousness and togetherness. And I am disappointed that I'm not living this dream.

—Kamel Daoud

Contents

CHAPTER 1

Where Was I?

"Time passes. Memory fades, memory adjusts, memory conforms to what we think we remember."

—Joan Didion

My sister Raghida looked at me.

"This is not supposed to happen to us."

A whole arc of a life contained in those few words, I thought. I started to say something but didn't.

Her husband Basil was sure he was going to live little short of forever. He made it to fifty-seven. To be a novice in this kind of pain, profound and boundless, is a gift from the gods—until it isn't. And now Raghida and my nieces were thrown into their first season of sorrow.

It was February 2011.

Arabs were beginning to rise like waves of surf. In the dead of winter, *Spring*, it seemed, had finally arrived in the Arab world. Now, alongside grief, there was anticipation and euphoria, the days an interplay of private wounds and collective furor, the clamor of a million voices in the background. The ramparts between the self and the infinite world beyond, those separations painstakingly erected to insulate and protect, all collapsed. I wanted to escape the moment and swim in it, to run and stay put, to cling to all my anchors and to coast, free and aimless.

There was much to say after the revolts, more to vent than to inform, I sometimes felt. I attempted my own fitful interpretations of the tumult in my *Thinking Fits* blog. For a long time, there was no respite. The family situation was raw, the stream of visuals breathtaking, the pace of events dizzying. And then dusk beckoned. Four years had passed since the first uprising, the region was heaving, fluid, mocking, and we in the family had only just begun our tentative peace with loss. I sensed that there was no better friend to rage than silence. That it was time for a kind of excavation.

It took a year of burrowing with my therapist to finally glimpse the instigators of my angst. Toward the end of our sessions, I asked the doctor if it was at all a coincidence that I chose to excavate my life as I was struggling to excavate *this Arab life*, with 2011 constantly staring at me in the rear-view mirror. It was the last note in my book of daily reflections that she had asked me to keep.

If you want to learn something about yourself in times of wholesale distress, to reconstruct the past and compose narratives of a present and a future that have become indescribable, the end result is a terrible loneliness. It's as if in the sweep of history the individual becomes beside the point; like a patient whose case is vital, groundbreaking even, but whose person is immaterial. But what's the sweep of history bereft of the lived moment? What is it without the warp and weft of human experience that weave a telltale story?

There are around forty million versions of me in the modern Levant: Jordanians and Palestinians, Syrians and Lebanese. By shared experience, we are many millions more. And by this measure alone, I am content to be identified as Arab, impatient though I am with the trappings of identity. But rare is the piece of nonfiction in which I can recognize myself as a Levantine, an Arab, with an enduring presence in these landscapes. Only novelists are nimble enough for this kind of needlework.

So, *This Arab Life* is my own kind of longing for storytelling—intimate, searching, in the moment. I wrote it to locate myself in this space, this place. I wrote it as a kind of introspection, a self-questioning about a matter that has long gnawed at me: the silence that descended on us Arabs in the 1980s, searing my generation and our children until the 2011 uprisings. And I wrote it to reach for daylight. Daylight. Sheer human determination to make sense of this new century seen only dimly as prancing silhouettes in the fog.

It's a tough chore depicting the temperament of a flailing Arab world.

In my journal, I catch myself dedicating to each shifting trend its own space—in pencil.

Once omnipresent regimes overwhelmed or fragmenting in every corner of the region.

A map that practically looks the same, a geography that is as disheveled as a teenager's closet.

Rising city-states.

Power haphazardly devolving from capital to province to town to village.

Massive population transfers within and across countries.

Ethnic and religious minorities and majorities interchangeable in their pain and the scale of their casualties.

Violence deregulated in a market of fear privatized and set free.

Islamic fundamentalism at war with itself, wounded now along with the Arab system that groomed it into stardom . . .

Young and old, moneyed or on the breadlines, antagonists and loyalists, activists and voyeurs, we now seesaw between anticipation and despondence, grasping at the familiar even as we curse it. When we are pressed for answers by friend and stranger alike, we demur, rehashing fleeting descriptions, much like amateur painters practicing in their sketchbooks.

Before 2011, we were always straining for guideposts. Are we truly a permanently subdued people, from Algeria to Syria? Does Islamism from the North African desert to the shores of the Mediterranean really claim our dreams and hearts? Is Palestine doomed to be forever lost to Israel? And we to foreign abuse? Does the ever widening void between rich and poor threaten no consequences for its architects? The glut of educated but unemployable youth; corruption and ineptitude; the cracked earth that threatens communal thirst; does none of this carry a risk for the mighty perched atop this pileup?

Those rumblings: the sit-ins by factory workers for better wages, the protests for economic and political reforms, the youthful restlessness that reveals itself in crusading digital apps and campaigns . . . Are they just random groans of discontent and resistance? And the most vexing question of them all: this stubborn resilience in us. How are we Arabs as a people able to persist in so many ways even as we suffer the catastrophic failures of the Arab State?

Then 2011 happened. We discovered that we could edit destinies written on our behalf. We discovered that our pain and yearnings transcend borders and chasms; that our fabric pulsates with color and verve. We discovered that dictatorship is not God and neither is Islamism. That politics is not dead. Nor is it instinctively violent. But with the passage of the years and the untold suffering unleashed, we came to understand as well the hard and never-ending struggle we face. Years into the 2011 outpourings, there are unexpected eruptions still. They are not so much a message of hope as they are a testimony to the energy of our upheaval under extremely unforgiving police states.

This Arab Life could be seen as a rather peculiar book. Problematic even. Writing that straddles genres is often called upon to shed all tongues but one. But that's not how this particular story wanted to be told. So, I gladly bowed to its wishes. And when I finally sat down to write it in 2018, there was a vague shape to my purpose, but there was no framework or notes or chapter outlines. I didn't know how I might begin and end it. There was no clue that I would be composing it in the midst of national trauma, a pandemic, and my own personal anguish. The book is inevitably faithful to the rush of my emotions, capturing the stream of my consciousness, but I freely acknowledge with gratitude those near and far who have influenced my work, those to whom I have regularly reached out to better understand *this Arab life.*

Who are we and who am I?

When I say "we," I am reminded of that definition by Sebastian Haffner in *Defying Hitler: A Memoir*: "We—that indefinite we, with no name, no party, no argument and no power."[1] I wish mine had the clarity of his. But it does not.

When I speak of "us" in the 2011 revolts, I am thinking more or less along the lines of Joel Beinin, my old Stanford professor: we are thus "a complex collage of striking workers, unemployed university graduates demanding work, human rights and democracy activists, demobilized leftists and Islamists. . .,"[2] and many sympathizers besides who joined or cheered from the sidelines when the people converged on the squares and streets. And obviously, *we* are like mercury, easily present in more than one category of actor. It reads like an unexceptional description of mobilized malcontents. And is that not revelatory about the universal nature, and ultimate vulnerability, of popular aspiration and grievance? Where I need to be more specific about which part of us I have in mind, I do so for clarity.

When I speak of "my" generation, I am referring to the one that came of political age in the 1980s. For us, every detail of this hour is especially poignant. So many of the vacuums that have become the hallmarks of our existence today began to show in our prime. Then, when we could see them, we called them signs and omens. Now we simply refer to them as "the way it is" or "the way we live."

To the question of "who am I?" I offer first some context and basic markers of identity. I am Lebanese born and Jordanian by circumstance. In 1962, when I was five months old, my family had to move to Jordan under political duress. We are five siblings: four sisters and one brother. I am the second youngest of the brood.

Courtesy of my father's hard work, we were and remain privileged. His was, as they say, a great ascent, through education and dogged ambition, from very modest means to a much more comfortable situation. And as he leapt, always busy, almost always on a plane, my mother took care of raising us day-to-day. I am often told that my bluntness is the work of her genes in me. I suspect it's rather more the way she brought us up.

I was educated in the US. I left earlier than my college-bound Jordanian friends to do my last two years of high school at Holton Arms in Maryland. I went to Georgetown University's Foreign Service School for my bachelor's degree (BS) and, three years later, to Stanford University for my master's degree (MS), where I studied international policy. My career has encompassed research, communication, and community development. In 2003, I made a conscious decision to devote more time to writing, much later than I would have liked. *This Arab Life* is my second book.

Our house was always very political. The Lebanese state's death sentence against my father in 1962 did nothing to dampen his passion for politics, nor ours. We were all, and remain still, secular to a fault. And, to varying degrees, we share liberal and nonconformist sensibilities. Religion, for us, has always been an accumulation of the folkloric rituals practiced informally by our elders. So the terms "Muslim" or "Shiite" are no more than labels used by others to define us.

This much about myself I concede easily. The rest of me, as it is for most people, is a much more tangled question. In attempting to answer it, I am particularly sensitive to Pankaj Mishra's counsel that "in every human case, identity turns out to be porous and inconsistent rather than fixed and discrete; and prone to get confused and lost in the play of mirrors."[3]

This Arab Life is, I believe, a testimony to the untethered self, even when still held by anchors, or in a straightjacket by lazy prejudice and stereotype. The book is an honest contemplation of these ballasts as well.

CHAPTER 2

Awkward Amities

Is it possible to recapture the light of the setting sun, or to hold a moment of joy that came and then departed? Can we bring back the storm, or freeze the waves of the sea and the raindrops as they fall from the sky?

—**Abd al-Rahman Munif,**
Story of a City

I was eleven and it was the summer of 1973. Jordan's King Hussein
had come for lunch in the upper restaurant of the Sports City.
In those days, el-Madineh, or the City, as we called it for short,
was life itself between June and September in Amman. It offered
opportunities for leisure, wellbeing, and culture within a sprawling
compound of greenery, swimming pools, restaurants, an amphitheater for plays and concerts, and courts for every imaginable sport.
There, after the 1970 bloody conflict between the Palestine Liberation Organization (PLO) and the Kingdom, we went to heal and be
carefree. There, we learned how to swim and dive and kiss; how to
play basketball, Trumps, ping-pong, and Truth or Dare. There, we
paraded in our shorts and bikinis, the boys in their Speedos, Mark
Spitz their hero. On the Roman-like amphitheater overlooking
thethree pools, the grass lawns, and the restaurants beyond we
sang to Paul Anka's "Papa," Charlie Rich's "The Most Beautiful
Girl," and Dolly Parton's "Jolene." On the grass, our hearts broke
only to flutter again. To this day, I have my membership card: 430.

Soon after lunch, the king appeared on the balcony, waved,
and then descended to take a stroll. The crowds went mad. The
young maidens in love, swooning with tears in their eyes, were
a sight to behold. I hadn't seen him in person before. His signed
photos to my father hung in our living room, though. I knew
that my family had a safe home in Jordan because of him. I knew
that, at his request, my father established the national airline
when he first decamped to Amman in 1962; that they shared a
passion for aviation; that they saw each other often. I knew all
this, but I didn't know the king.

Author's Sports City membership card 430, 1972.

From left: Wasfi Tal; Toufiq Tabbaa'; author's father, Ali; King Hussein; and Abd al-Ghani Abu Quora, 1965.

A multitude immediately formed around the Hashemite monarch and his bodyguards. As was his habit, he was all ease, twinkles, and smiles. I was still very short then and scrawny. I slinked my way in between hips and thighs and found myself right beside him. We strode together for a while as the mob jostled us left and right, and every time he reached out to shake someone's hand, I planted my own first in his palm. I swaggered for the rest of that afternoon in triumph.

That day at el-Madineh occupies the very first page in my journal. There is an old home movie feel to that memory—a two-minute, silent clip of bygone years. This was not my intention. Regret more than nostalgia, if you ask me, as if I am freezing history in one scene, in the hope that it might suggest a truth much larger than its tiny self. I have many of these: a thick album of rueful "once-upon-a-times."

This was Jordan when I was eleven, it was summer, and the king and I swayed at the Sports City for what felt like an eternity. The way things were to the accompaniment of a string quartet. They tug at my heart, these "once-upon-a-times," not because of the passage of time and the vanishing of an old world that was supposedly better, but because when I look back, I realize that what I lived and loved was just one scenario that had lost out to others. And I wonder to myself, what role had I played in this unforgivable lapse?

I need a whole vocabulary of the heart to conjure myself in that Jordan of the 1970s, but my therapist tells me I have none. There is no *I* in my stories, only *it*.

"You're a woman without a voice," she says. Surprised, I timidly volunteer that those who know me would be mystified by her observation.

"No, they wouldn't. You are very generous with your surroundings, with others, to the minutest detail. But you're an absolute miser about yourself."

She hands me a list of basic emotions. It's a humbling moment. I bite my lower lip and ask, "Back to first grade?"

Happy. Serene. Contented. Tickled Pink... I begin. I notice my eyes are drawn to the middle of the list. I start to hover around *Ecstatic, Euphoric, Thrilled*, but I'd have had to smoke some really *Zippy* stuff to be this *Overjoyed* for that long, even in the Amman of the '70s.

The thing is, *I* can, *I* do, still feel them down to my bones, those years. They enveloped *my* Amman much like a mother cuddles her newborn. But, how can *I*, "a woman without a voice," describe this embrace to my therapist with words that only the heart knows how to utter? Shall I paint her a picture?

The quietude punctured only by the turn of my bicycle wheels; the early evening chirps of crickets as I nestled on the couch to watch Mighty Mouse and Betty Boop; the faint whoosh of a car turning into our side street in idyllic Shmeisani, our neighborhood; the laughter bouncing off my school walls; our neighbors' balconies; through the grass fields of my Sports City; our garden's trees and leaves.

"Are these images close enough to the gurgling sounds in a mother's womb?" I ask her in my journal. "Do they explain why I felt so *Contented* and *Serene*? Can you hear my voice in them?"

The truth is I cruised for what seemed like forever on *Giddy*. Amman was one long lullaby if you were more or less middle class, middlebrow, and generally kept to the safe side of the road. It was a study in restraint, diffident architecture, and mild living. It could never compete with its neighbor Beirut, supine like a courtesan on the Mediterranean Sea, long the haunt of hipsters, merchants, troublemakers, and spooks. But Amman never cared to compete. For most of its visitors, especially Beirutis, it was the dead sound of slumber and yawns. Daylight was the crawl of snails, nighttime the calm of the countryside, human shadows in faintly lit living rooms, the glare of TV screens until 11 p.m., when the national anthem played behind a picture of King Hussein. Our favorite Arab show was *Sah al-Nawm*, a Syrian political and social parody; our favorite drama, *Rich Man, Poor Man*, the best American import. The BBC's riveting *World at War* was the must-see of the week.

For years after the 1970–71 Civil War, keys turned in their locks by 10 p.m.

Entertainment was mostly behind closed doors. Itching for a wild night out, the only destinations we had were Villa Rosa and Cezar with live bands and all. For quieter evenings, Ali Baba or Abu Ahmad offered Arabic cuisine, the Intercontinental Hotel and Leonardo da Vinci a continental menu. Ours was a cocoon at its most snug. And as with cocoons everywhere, a fleeting moment felt deceptively eternal.

I happened recently upon Abd al-Rahman Munif's *Story of a City* about his childhood in 1940s Jordan. I didn't know that the

Iraqi-Saudi novelist grew up there. His Amman is speckled with places and names and streets, with laughter and shenanigans so wonderfully familiar. In the thirty years between his childhood and mine, little had changed in our city, even though it had borne the brunt of the 1948 and 1967 Palestinian catastrophes, even though it had grown in population from 30,000 in 1943 to 429,000 in 1972, and even though it had spread well beyond the Duwwar al-Awal, or 1st Roundabout, in Jabal Amman, which had been the outer limit of Munif's world.

As far as our eyes could see, nothing seemed out of sync in Amman, even when it was. Not in Jabal al-Weibdeh, nor in Jabal al-Hussein, nor yet in Jabal Amman, the old neighborhoods of the city sitting on top of three of the capital's seven hills, which were my universe. Nothing out of the ordinary in the ever-so-quiet suburb of Shmeisani where I lived. Nothing amiss at the 1st, 2nd, 3rd, or 4th Duwwar around which we cruised on endless afternoons: a noisy procession of male serenades and female gushes. Nothing was odd about the el-Madineh of those magical postwar years. Nor about the decent, orderly roads, or the pretty one-floor houses, or the congregation of buildings downtown, most no more than four stories tall. And certainly nothing was unusual about the Tabbaa' villa in the 4th Duwwar, the city's rare nod to luxury, along with the grand Bilbeisi house downtown.

So it was with Amman's six leading schools, all legacies of the missionaries' zeal that educated the rising bourgeoisie. Among them was my Orthodoxieh (National Orthodox School), Jordan's only co-educational institution then. For the boys, Mutran (Bishop's School), De La Salle Frères, and Terra Sancta; for the girls, Rosary College School, Ahliyeh (CMS, Evangelical School), and Lady of Nazareth. The Islamic Scientific College, between the 1st and 2nd Duwwar, which offered an education with an Islamic flavor, didn't feel out of place either. Nor did the other hills, where Amman's less comfortable lived, and the refugee camps that were the stuff of heartbreak. Amman was not a city that could hide its flaws. None of us, young or old, and certainly not me, were unaware of its darker side. The city was too small, its ordeals too present and too raw. But how we felt about them was a different matter entirely.

Jordan just felt like a country that could tiptoe through thorn fields. Its frictions had claws, but they didn't appear to cut too deep. Ties of kinship, Bedouin loyalties and rituals, crosses and minarets, all flirted tentatively with the seductions of modernity. In Amman, an awkward amity existed between God, bathing suits, and whisky. The city, for a very long time, entertained a whole medley of accommodations: between Jordanian and Palestinian; between Arab and Jordanian; between the pull of the outside and the reserve of the inside; between poor and rich, rural and urban, west of the city and its east . . . At least this is how it seemed to me, and many others besides. There, on the fragile surface of life, where children played and grown-ups went about the business of their day, subterranean tensions were mostly conveyed in gestures and whispers, winks and taunts.

For a small, upstart country whose main charge was to improve the odds of its survival in a dog-eat-dog Levant, this was no mean feat. The pressures called for a routine of brawls and fistfights. Not that we didn't have those: restlessness, failed coups d'état, and both botched and successful assassination plots pockmarked the 1950s and '60s. But Jordan had a knack for sneaking around its discords and discomforts, its insecurities and intolerances. When blood flowed in 1970, it seemed out of character. And when it stopped soon after, we quickly tagged the episode a force majeure triggered by intruders on our politics. If this was not entirely true, there was certainly enough truth in it to satisfy us, and we moved on.

For all the warmth that suffused my childhood, I did have my own share of mild discomforts in my adopted country. I felt them every so often when I would hear "hatha el-libnani" (that Lebanese) whispered about my father. And there was the time when my sister Raghida fought with her tenth grade Islamic Religion teacher at the CMS who claimed that Shiites worshipped fire. But perhaps an incident in primary school best describes the ease with which we lived with our awkward amities: when the teacher wanted to split us into Christians and Muslims for religious instruction classes, I stood lost in the middle, not knowing to which side I should march.

"Ghandour, to the right—with the Muslims," she thundered. We all laughed.

I felt unease every time I saw Umm (mother of) Mohammad, our Palestinian housekeeper. A portrait of pain and patience, her entire being an expression of bad luck and injustices: Abu (father of) Mohammad dead; Mohammad himself, a wretch; Palestine gone. She couldn't have been older than forty, always clad in her traditional *thawb* and loose white *mandeel* that draped over her head like a shawl. On her warm face, sparkling beads for eyes set on a bed of creases and wrinkles, I could not help but trace the woes of the 1948 and '67 wars: the loss of homeland and the uprooting of family trees. I remember the same unease when, at the end of her working day, we would drive her back to the Wihdat Refugee Camp, a world away but no more than 15 minutes by car from us in Shmeisani.

Even that shimmering summer's day at the Sports City back in 1973 with King Hussein had its own very special awkward amity. I can see the last clip, before the old reel races to its end: a lingering finale at once adult and childlike. As I dance around on the grass, happy and full of myself, I glimpse, sitting propped up with their arms back at an angle, my two best friends watching me impassively. I stop as I register their silence, not sullen, not angry, just vaguely hesitant, unimpressed. That was the first time I understood, however crudely, that I was a daughter of the regime and, strictly speaking, they were not.

As I sit here ages older, I cannot say that I recognized these stains on a blissful past as malignant or prophetic. They didn't feel quite right to me, but then neither did they represent harbingers of dire things. Maybe they should have.

I would have liked these first few pages to evoke more than the state of my effervescence. I would have liked them, for example, to be more generous with Jordan's 1970–71 bloodletting.

Family shortly after arrival in Jordan in 1962. Children from left: Fadi, Raghida, Amal.

It was fratricide, after all. But that would be cheating—the older me muscling in on the little girl's joy. The truth is that any apprehensions I had back then were mere faint blemishes on the otherwise perfect face of my adolescence. An adolescence that remarkably seemed to overcome my own family's history. Because even at eleven, I was not personally naïve about politics or unaware of its brutal temperament. This consciousness was practically written into my DNA. My father was sentenced to death by the Lebanese state in 1962. My Lebanese family ended up as political refugees in Jordan that same year.

It was October when my mother, in flight, reached the Lebanese crossing. We were four in tow: Raghida, six; my brother Fadi, three; my paternal aunt Najah, and me, barely five months old. In the rush to escape, my mother had not had time to get me an ID card.* She remembers the border quiet, the Lebanese soldier gentle. When he politely declined to let us out, Raghida started pulling frantically at my mother's dress, crying, "They're going to take us to prison." The soldier felt sorry for us and stamped us through. Jordan, from that second onward, became our home.

---

*My oldest sister Asma, who was twelve at the time, also didn't have an ID and so stayed behind in Beirut for a few months with my maternal grandmother.

I always thought that, tucked well inside my mother's womb and later as a baby when she packed us all up and escaped, that I had been spared the worst of her jitters and agonies; that what intuitive insight I had developed about politics I had formed free of the emotional turmoil that attached to memory. All my life I thought that drama was my sister's thing. She had earned it. She was old enough. She had heard. She had seen. The death sentence, the surreptitious messages, the hushed dread, the hectic arrangements. Dear family friends who became strangers. Strangers who were saviors.

All this time, I thought that by pure chance of timing I had ducked Raghida's nightmares. I was wrong.

Today, I watch aghast as millions are chased out of Syria and Iraq, and I wonder how many of us in the Arab world *sotto voce* became political refugees over the past sixty years. Not in droves because of sectarian cleansing or civil strife or coups d'état or invasions, but in trickles, in mortal fear of wrathful regimes. How many fleeing fathers instructed their wives, as my father did his, to gather the children and head for another country? With some effort, we could accurately estimate those who languished in prison or died under torture or disappeared altogether or were gunned down. Estimating those who made it to safety is impossible.

Politics is very personal for us Arabs. I say this with sweeping ease, because it has that kind of intimate reach. I cannot think of one person I know who has not been somehow hurt or sullied by it.

Our tale is something of a multi-generational saga, a dizzying one hundred years of *Sturm und Drang* in the Middle East: to my grandparents went the traumas of famine, world war, new masters, new borders and nationalities; to my parents went the alluring prospect of a future unshackled by colonialism, fast followed by the post-independence agitations and ferments of the 1950s and 1960s; to my older siblings went the 1970s, the student demonstrations and strikes, as if the last gasp of an era of squandered possibilities. To me, to us all, belonged the silence, a generation rendered mute by a cavalcade of betrayals and defeats, none more shattering than 1967.

We were too young to fathom the magnitude of that rout in six mornings and nights. But the torment was ours all the same. The rest of Palestine, west of the river, was lost and with it the Arab dream of return: return of the land, and with it the vanquishing of humiliation and shame. I myself have but one tattered memory of Jericho. I can see it, in the Jordan Valley, maybe toward the end of 1966. The hotel where my parents used to take us on Friday, the official day off. Raghida, ten, and me, four, standing in front of the carved façade of white horses as the camera went click. My mother asked me the other day if I didn't at all remember Madam Na'oum's Lebanese restaurant in Ramallah. Alas, I don't. That photo is my only keepsake of Palestine.

And, of course, there were lingering tears on many a believer's cheek. No wonder '67 was very quickly processed, packaged, and stamped as the *Naksa* (the Setback). It was one thing for Egypt's bumbling King Farouq to botch it all up in the first round in 1948—commonly referred to as the *Nakba* (the Catastrophe)—quite another for the heroic officer Gamal Abdel Nasser, who toppled him and soon after became Egypt's president and savior, to be all but flattened the second time around.

Our official lexicons were, in this way, manipulated. How else might history be tricked into a kinder verdict by "revolutionary" states that rose from the ineptitude of the old "reactionary" ones? Not that it much helped fudge the dawning certainties: '67 became for all of us, apostates and apostles alike, the year of the great flood. We have life before '67, a filigree of aspirations, myths, and messiahs, and life after '67: not a single fable or hero in the house. All for the mop! From then on, dogmas, bullies, peddlers, and their kiosks.

And so, there is nothing in my family's past, nothing in that era, that should have encouraged me to be so heedlessly happy. Certainly not so soon after Jordan's 1970 Civil War. A clash between the PLO—the debut, if you like, for the non-state actor of the day—and a young monarchy that bored into communities and aborted their delicate sense of belonging.

In a matter of months, hundreds would die on the Jordanian army's side, thousands between fighters and civilians on the side of the PLO and Palestinians. The physical damage was not limited for such a swift joust, but the hardest hits, as it would turn out, were mostly to the soul of the country. The refugee camps took the heaviest blows. For the next fifty years, play, rewind, repeat, wherever they lived, encircled much like prison colonies by their local hosts.

Few were mere bystanders in this spectacle of human folly. Few would emerge unscathed. And, most meaningfully for us in Jordan, few realized the degree to which it would write Jordan's future course.

Of the morning after, I clutch at the haziest of memories. Yasser Arafat loses his bet and heads for Lebanon with his men. Jordan's Prime Minister Wasfi Tal falls, murdered by Black September, a Palestinian paramilitary group, on the floor of Cairo's Sheraton Hotel. We huddled in the evening, glued to the screen as thousands of men in red and white *hatta w 'igal** swarm the coffin and their king. I think Beethoven's Fifth was playing. They always played it in official funerals. I cried.

Why, then, the sparkle of '73? I can't be sure forty-five years on. It could well have been my instinct to conceal distress, to build my own little protective silo. To be both Arab and sanguine. The kingdom was burying its traumas, my family had overcome its own, so the child in me must have been only too happy to mimic those who saw things I didn't see and knew things I didn't know.

My father, Ali, wanted to name me Nidal (Struggle), one of those many Arabic names whose resonance is lost in translation. My mother, Altaf, insisted on Amal (Hope). He wanted the trench-

---

*The Jordanian headdress. The Palestinian headdress is black and white.

es. She yearned for the light. He thought his couldn't possibly have meaning without hers. She won. Besides, when she had me, he was on the run, and I was one of four clinging to her.

If, in the wake of calamity and bedlam, all we could do as children was to catch the tail end of furious arguments and parrot the sentiments and sensibilities of our elders, then hope it must have been for me. For us. Because I know I was not alone.

That, I suppose, was the miracle of the Hashemite monarchy in those years: reassuring its flock that all is not lost, when, in fact, much of it was. That Jordan may be poorly endowed, that its designated role may be as permanent custodian of Palestinians cast out of Palestine, but at least it had King Hussein who, for all his faults, was the best man to watch over it. When we, his flock, looked around us, at Syria and Iraq, at Saudi Arabia, at Egypt down south, even Lebanon in the north, we felt rather satisfied with our lot. Under this Hashemite, then, a temperate future for Jordan was not altogether far-fetched.

When asked, we could point to any one of our good fortunes: good schools, clean air, clear roads, steady hand above, secure streets below, unlocked doors at night, the Sports City for fun, virginal Aqaba on the Red Sea for the beach. On a mere 89,000 square kilometers, history, ancient and new, had left all manner of monuments and relics, some all glory and grace, others all ruin and pain. No oil, no gas, no minerals to speak of, no strategic canals and trade routes, just a tiny Jordan, rich in sorrow and sand and beauty. Whenever we had our doubts, we looked around us some more and agreed that Jordan, awkward amities and all, was not such a bad place after all.

And so, there again on the surface of our world was the distinct whiff of renewal, and yes, hope. A country that had been amputated in '67, only to plunge into a frightening communal squabble three short years later, had survived and was still young enough to reimagine itself. If that's what it really wanted.

It didn't. It could have, but it didn't.

❖ ❖ ❖ ❖

There is a longing and lament in every thought about my Amman. And so, too, about my Beirut. I prop them up, much like mirrors, and I see reflections of our bewildering descent from youthful promise to senescent fatigue. On them hangs the weight of my dejection. But I take solace from Abd al-Rahman Munif's words about the profound meaning of the city to its children:

> *A city is life in all its various permutations. It is places, people, trees, the smell of rain, the earth and time itself in a state of flux. A city is its people's way of perceiving things: how they talk, how they dealt with events, how they faced and how they transcended them. A city is the dreams and disappointments that filled minds and hearts, those dreams which came true and those which were frustrated, leaving in their wake wounds and scars.*
>
> *A city is its people's moments of happiness and sadness.*
> *A city is the way in which it welcomed those it loved,*
> *and confronted those who were its enemies.*[1]

CHAPTER 3

The Age
of the Whisper

At a lecture, Cairo University student to Hassan al-Banna, the founder of the Muslim Brotherhood who passed away in 1949: "What is acceptable art in Islam?"

Hassan al-Banna: "Acceptable art is acceptable; and forbidden art is forbidden."

Every once in a while, an old black and white film or yellowing photograph of Cairo, Beirut, Alexandria, Damascus, Amman, Jerusalem, or Baghdad in the 1920s, '30s, or '50s surfaces on Facebook. An emoji race ensues between the red heart and the teary-eyed smiley face, as a barrage of clicks unleashes a collective digital sigh.

All very sweet, of course. Death's cruel separations are bridged, however momentarily, and the bygone past and its dwellers are summoned from the beyond. There's something distinctly poignant about my generation's ritual, as if we are mourning a life once richly lived that has been all but expunged. It is not so much nostalgia for our own youth—most of these images are of a time before ours—more a lamentation for vast disruption and irretrievable loss. Of the orphans we are.

I often experience this same feeling of abandonment whenever my mother drops an old vignette into our conversations. One afternoon a few years ago, we sat talking about the garbage bin that Sidon had become. This southern city had produced three billionaire prime ministers after the 1975–1990 Civil War. As I bemoan the ugly concrete that mars the town, the trash mountains that threaten the Mediterranean's ecosystem, the blackened waters that surround Sidon's floating citadel, the filth that litters its inner streets, she offers me this consolation: "In the old days, on our way to Nabatiyeh,* we would always know that we were approaching Sidon from the scent of the orange blossoms."

---

*My mother's hometown further south.

Author's mother, Altaf, on her honeymoon in Istanbul, 1955.

In all fairness to Sidon, very few towns in Lebanon, including Nabatiyeh, have managed to escape the downward slide from delicately perfumed orange blossom to stinking cesspit. Very little of the integrity of our mountains, of the entire western sea-board and anything in between has been spared. What beauty remains intact for us and our children, so pleasing to the starved eye, stands ground like pink lotuses in a swamp.

Everywhere else in the Arab world, it's a variation on the same theme. To those who knew the younger face of Arab cities, there is very little in them they would recognize. The story is no different across oceans and continents; in man-made reckless change, the Middle East is by no means the worst offender. Harrowing tales of vengeance and the plundering of natural resources abound. Wherever the finger lands on a rotating globe, spoliation is everywhere; it's merely a matter of scale.

But talking about the environment is way above my pay grade. I have barely enough self-confidence to whisper about the meaning of our own erasures and silence: the astonishing meanness and carelessness with which we have torn into our continuities, those connections that preserve heritage and collective memory; the creeping acquiescence and mediocrity that have permitted prolonged and wholesale violence. When we click away at our emojis, it is not the appalling mutilations that we bemoan, but the ubiquitous ruptures in society, politics, and culture that have made such mauling unexceptional. All it takes is a chronology of postcards and a mother's wistful reminiscences to retrieve the missing parts of our severely diminished identity.

The unmistakable tragedy in this copious archive of failure and rape is that virtually all of it is relatively recent. So, I ask myself, what have we done? What sin have we committed? I ask not in astonished atonement, but as a point of departure for a very difficult conversation that explores that gnarled expanse called the self and the period that defined it.

I look back on the three decades that closed the last century and I am gripped by how dejected we were for a generation so young, and yet how awake we were to the fact of it. How thoroughly atomized our life was the minute we stepped out of the house, our passions and ambitions and expectations nurtured in subconscious dugouts. It's as if we were islands unto ourselves, not so much isolated but apart, alone. Not disengaged but resigned. Not without ideals but without the essential belief that in the larger, and often intimidating scheme of things, we actually count; that the way of things was tenacious, immovable, and much stronger than our desire for it to give way.

I am struck too by how well the smothered anxieties of this inner self mirrored those of the world around it: thirty uninspired years at once fitful and placid. The fury of events, the quietude of the spirit. Invasions, fratricides, assassinations, plots by old comrades foiled, a rebelling brother unmasked, sporadic bread riots in capitals, chemical weapons and massacres in the countryside, all fizzing like firecrackers in the long, dark night. A calendar in bumps, blows, and thuds: an Arab-Israeli war (1973), civil war in Lebanon (1975–1990), the first Israeli invasion of Lebanon (1978), the Israeli siege of Beirut (1982), trouble in Saudi Arabia (1979), in Egypt (1977, 1981,

1986), in Syria (1979–1984), in Tunisia (1984), in Sudan (1985, 1989), in Iraq (1979, 1984, 1988), in Yemen (1986), in Jordan (1970, 1976, 1986, 1989), between Iraq and Iran (1980–1988), between Iraq and Kuwait (1990–1991), the first intifada in Palestine (1987) . . . And so it went on, past 1991.

But I cannot lie. I recall angst, not alarm. The tumult, for us, was par for the course, the normal in the abnormal if you like, except for one jolt that transfixed us all. The downfall of the Iranian Shah, Mohammad Reza Pahlavi, in 1979. Our presidents and kings died of natural causes, or were forced out by bullet or coup, but toppled by the people? Not in our lifetime. In 1969, Col. Muammar Gaddafi deposed King Muhammad Idris bin Muhammad al-Mahdi as-Senussi. In 1970, Hafez Assad forced out Salah Jadid in Syria, Abdel Nasser's heart stopped in Egypt, and Sultan Qaboos deposed his father, Said Bin Taimur, in Oman. Saudi Arabia's King Feisal was dispatched by his nephew in 1975. But the Shah! His people rose, emperor and people fought, blood flowed, and, lo and behold, he fell!

Nothing happened on this side of the sea, though. In my youth, there were no mass occupations of squares, no demonstrations blanketing boulevards and side streets, no nationwide strikes and shutdowns. We just listened and watched as spectators from our rooftops and living rooms. For all the noise from our crises, in the end, the political status quo still shrieked loudest.

Why the Iranians and not us? It's hard to imagine that the question didn't make the rounds in our sitting rooms; certainly in those of our beloved sovereigns. But the awe! That I remember. The unthinkable creeping in through the back door while all eyes were fixed on the front porch. What fun, the people sniggered. What next, wondered those reigning over them.

Riveting theater, Iran. How could it not be? The characters alone prefigured the *Game of Thrones*: the comically imperious Reza Pahlavi as Shahenshah (King of Kings); the tragically misguided Shahbanu (Queen Consort) Farah Deeba as his wife; the cartoon-sinister Ashraf as his twin sister; the urbane, rose-in-the-lapel Hoveyda as prime minister; the frozen scowler Khomeini as the Night King; SAVAK's men as the bad guys; Abolhassan Bani Sadr,

Sadegh Ghotbzadeh et al. as the good ones.* And towering above the entire cast, as threatening to Khomeini's plans as he was to the Shah, the revolution's true ideologue: the screamingly charismatic, faintly sorrowful Ali Shariati, who expired at the age of forty-four just nine months before 1978's spark.

The frenzied myth-making in Tehran was so loud that you could hear it all the way in Amman. There were stories about tortures and rapes in prison at SAVAK's hands; about the cities' revolutionaries massing with the rural poor for freedom against an American stooge; about the thousands upon thousands of dead the revolution declared as its martyrs.

It would take an assortment of revisionist researchers over decades to sober up intoxicated minds and disentangle fact from rumor from fib from fiction. Those keen on the disentangling found that, according to the theocracy's own revised numbers, the alleged 50,000 martyred by the Shah's guns were, in fact, between 744 and 895;[1] that the purportedly formidable army was actually dispirited and feeble; that SAVAK was by the region's standards quite the walk in the park, more a den of demoralized, bungling, and disloyal men than a fearsome praetorian guard and network of torturers and spies;[2] that, when it came down to it, the Shah was rather easy pickings, the prickliest of courtiers to the ficklest of patrons, the weakest of kings and the most paper-like of Middle Eastern tigers. Not that I would presume to minimize the epic victory or its cataclysmic nature. Far from it. This is just a footnote about why the Shah was much easier to overthrow in 1979 than our modern Arab dynasts then and now.

Absent the domino effect, soon enough Iran stopped being much of a pastime. We all quickly figured that, as usual, if Arab heads were going to roll, an adventurous type at the top would wield the sword. But somewhere along the way wisdom became conventional and lazy, and turned into a stale truism: that the only change worth noting is the one at the pinnacle

---

*SAVAK was Iran's intelligence service. Bani Sadr was Iran's first elected president after the revolution until he was impeached by Parliament in 1980. Sadeg Ghotbzadeh was foreign minister from 1979 to 1980. He was executed in 1982.

of power. Without ever really meaning to, we started holding tight to this cliché. We witnessed in bemusement the insidious transformations that slowly chipped away at our way of life and foretold the changing face of an Arab world that we all had thought immovable.

Day by day, fault lines were multiplying, class disparities were wider, impoverished thinking was flourishing, education was failing, politics was becoming an inane insider game, as governments transformed into ever worse versions of their previous selves. The effect on us was physical, conspicuous.

In the 1970s, in Amman, we went to Cinema Bassman downtown. In the 1980s, we (the haves) didn't. In the 1970s, hole-in-the-wall Hashem was for those early morning falafel and hummus binges after a hard night. By the 1990s, it wasn't.

In my old school, Orthodoxieh, I had absolutely no clue in the 1970s which of my classmates was there on a scholarship, and only the very wealthy stood out, not because they meant to, but because the rest of us sat, more or less, on the same rung. Came the 1990s, we knew which schools were for the lower middle class, which for the middle class, and which for the much better off.

With all this came a whole new catalogue of nervous signals among people dealing across chasms, the etiquettes of strangers in foreign lands. At the Sports City of the 1970s, the habits inside were little different from the ones outside for Amman's middle class. The easy mixing between men and women, girls and boys, the dress codes unencumbered by religious dictates and cultural wars, the comfort in one's choices with little fear of harassment or backlash. Today, there are notes online cautioning women that el-Madineh is not particularly welcoming.

The sidewalks of Amman were near faultless in the 1970s. By the 1990s, they were every length, width, and height. In the 1970s, Palestine still made you half-raving, half-incensed; in the 1980s, it played tricks on you, at once fiery and hopeless; by 2001, it left you mystified and numb. Our water supply was barely adequate in the '70s. By the mid-1990s, it was a crisis. Today, Jordan is one of the five most water-scarce countries on this planet.

Change, sometimes incremental and surreptitious, sometimes loud and obnoxious, was acutely felt and quietly endured. Of course, there was no transformation quite like Islam's, as stubborn as it was protean, as intimidating as it was alluring. Sheikhs became sentries, teachers turned into preachers, schools became mosques, mosques became schools. There were dos and don'ts for every occasion, all reminding us, in case we were not smart enough to get the glaring point, that *Islam Is the Solution*. On paper it all looked a bit frothy and harebrained, in practice it was greedy and insatiable.

I remember our knee-jerk reactions to the Muslim Brotherhood's encroachments on our lives, starting in our teens. Islam's place at school used to be only in the Islamic Religion class. Enter the Muslim Brotherhood (MB) into the Ministry of Education in the early '70s, and Islam began infiltrating practically every textbook. In 1976, the Ministry, with barely a whimper, threw out philosophy. In my teens, the Muezzin's call to prayer was just that; in my twenties, he was blaring down venom at me day and night, doomsday like. For the better part of the '70s, women's looks and wardrobes mixed and mingled. I did not know and barely saw a single veiled woman. By the end of the decade, the streets were fast becoming catwalks for Islamist garb.

Veiling was not a matter of class or education or address. Not in Amman. In this, my childhood was little different from Munif's. The inhabitants of the tiny city in the 1940s, many of them Circassian Muslims, simply didn't have veiling in their rituals. "The first impression that a tourist passing through Amman during the 1940s. . .would have had was that the city was experiencing a constant carnival because the variety in costumes, accents and traditions was greater than anywhere else."[3] And then there came a time when it would all begin to change. For Islamists, it was really a straightforward affair. They just massaged lore into doctrine. None of it was truly alien or foreign, much of it was helpfully accompanied by social services for the neglected and forgotten, and all of it was grimly cast as the immutable word and will of God, the better to induce the hush of the graveyard. Slowly (bit by bit, not all of a sudden, not out of the blue, not overnight), veiling, once a gesture of female modesty, turns into a duty, and a handshake between a man and a woman, long an unfussy business, becomes a sin. Once comfortably settled into the rank and file of the Ministry of Education, it was easy for the MB to mold the minds of successive generations. To them as well went control over the personal status laws to shape gender relations, obligations, and rights. The Kingdom may have ceded all this ground in a fit of absentmindedness, or to reward a reliable ally, or to mollify a prickly junior partner intent on spreading their gospel. Whatever the reason(s), the gift was the very character of us.

A bird's-eye view of a long and winding tale, one might say. That seems a little ungenerous of me. Over forty years have passed since those early days when the wind blew and entire landscapes swayed to its incessant rhythms. It has become customary, and with good reason, to identify the 1979 Iranian Revolution and the subsequent 1979 Siege of Mecca by al-Jamaa al-Salafiya al-Muhtasiba (JSM), a Salafi Jihadist group, as watersheds in the Middle East's escalating politics of sectarianism and Islamist radicalism. But for us, the minutiae of the region's changing moods were being felt before Khomeini landed in Tehran in February 1979 and Mohammad Abdullah al-Qahtani, Juhayman al Outaybi, and their followers attacked Mecca's Masjid al-Haram in November of the same year.

I often imagine the period as a museum of images and symbols of a contested history. So many of them, and so much to write about. But for me, the veil has the most honored place in this imaginary gallery. This is not because it's the best expression of the rise of Islamic fundamentalism, as its Islamist champions and Western critics insist it is, but because it evokes so well our existential disquiets as a people.

In truth, I would be insulting the veil if I give all the credit to Islamists for spreading it with such vigor. To freeze it in time, as they have, is to deny the mercurial role it has played since it was dubbed our identity's crown as women. The glory of the hijab, in fact, belongs to all of us—Muslim "Brothers" and "Sisters," mothers and fathers, systems and peoples, East and West.

I am actually in awe of the veil. That's why I have chosen it as my lantern in illuminating our muddy cultural terrains. Paradoxically, it is conformist and revolutionary, oppressive and liberating, spontaneous and premeditated, uncovering the fault lines that have long fractured Arab society. It both feeds and flouts every stereotype, celebrates and mocks submission, announces surrender and declares war, is a tormentor and a savior. It all depends on the woman wearing it and her circumstances. Among my own friends and colleagues, from Cairo all the way to Tripoli via Damascus and Amman, those who willingly don it, who wear and hate it, and those who wore it and then finally took it off, every conceivable reason is mentioned: because Islam tells me to, the family forces me to, my dear father implores me to, because I would look odd in my neighborhood, because this is my emancipation from Western temptation, because this is my revolt against imperialism, because I am tired of being sexually harassed everywhere I go, because it's the price I have to pay to go to school or work. . . .

Therefore, to pigeonhole the hijab as purely an Islamist cipher is to censor all its meanings but one. And the thorniest of these meanings is that of freedom of choice in smothered societies constantly negotiating over it. In this sense, the success of this piece of cloth, beyond perhaps anything Islamism could have hoped for, is an eloquent commentary on the fraught path of women in public space, and the compromises we have had to make to ensure our continued presence there. The hijab, in point of fact, has been the most vivid demonstration of our struggle to engage. And we have, as part of this quest, wrapped ourselves in it in order to unshackle the rest of our being in a wary world ever mistrustful of us. I say this because ours is a Middle East awash with complaints about the unfair challenges of modern times, internal and foreign, political and social, real and contrived. And we women have been conveniently chosen by a patriarchal culture as the showcase of its resilience, its battle for honor and authenticity. We women are at once the measure of success in this "civilizational" tussle with modernity and the scapegoats for failure everywhere else. And so, we "wear" this role, this cover, as a burden or a privilege, as a penalty or a duty, as an albatross or a pass, as a mere gesture or a statement about identity—even, increasingly, as a confident dialogue with modernity itself.

In my own family, Zeinab (Umm Ali), my paternal grandmother, wore the traditional long white *mandeel*; Mira (Umm Mussbah), my maternal grandmother, the short, modern écharpe that rested midway up her hair. Of the two, Zeinab was the more modest one; Mira always walked out of the house in dresses just below the knee and splendid high heels. My mother tells me that she, at the age of nine, was expected to wear a scarf, like all her friends in Nabatiyeh. Girls and women were also in the habit of wearing a transparent silk face covering when they went to town. Only the wives of sheikhs wore the chador,

Umm Mussbah and Asma, author's
grandmother and eldest sister, 1951.

the more conservative full black garb and head cover. Only the daughters of Dr. Bahij Mirza recused themselves from all such dress codes; no one dared to criticize them because he was very respectable and his girls were as feisty as they come. My mother used to wear her headscarf on the way to school, hide it under the apricot tree, and put it on again on her way back home in the afternoon. By her early teens, it was shoved ever deeper into her closet. By the time she joined her mother and father in Africa in 1947, when she was sixteen, it had disappeared altogether. The rest of us Ghandour women—daughters, granddaughters, nieces, and cousins—never wore the hijab, never wanted to, and were never expected to.

But whatever the motivations of the wearer, the hijab is here to stay. It may continue to reign supreme or it may yet again become just one of many ordinary sights on a busy street. It all depends on whether younger generations of Arabs are finally ready to let go of it as a totem of honor and resilience, releasing all of us women with it as their weapon of choice.

These were the trends that loomed as we were approaching adulthood: the push and shove between a people whose acquiescence was more grudging than genuine, and an Arab state at once omnipotent and chronically insecure. The sparring between ideas, the scuffles between creeds, and the back and forth between sages in the public sphere, all now a deafening peep. "Journalist" became synonymous with mouthpiece. Academic quarterly publications, mostly defunct by the end of their first year, kept up a nominal fight, touting positions and thoughts, some sponsored by regimes, some not. If you sought culture at its most daring, you went underground; at its safest, you read books and went to art galleries. The empty bombast alone told of dogmas and their political parties becoming little more than sing-alongs; of trade unions bartering away their workers' rights.

We had reached a state of catharsis. First went the prospect of real independence and freedom; then the lionized ideologies that promised them; then Palestine itself; on its heels the demigods and icons; trailing all of them the dreams. The emptiness was all that was left. The desert. And the silence. The arena was swept clean, except for one aspiration, one perfect enemy: Islamism. The stage was set: the state and them, love and hate in a broken, hollowed-out Arab house.

It was the Age of the Whisper, of pragmatism, and so we went about the business of living pragmatically. If we absolutely had to reach for something larger than our individual self, our choice was between religion and family, or, more often, a potent mélange of both. Those who wanted a totally clean break went to Europe and the US. Those who wanted to make serious money went to the Gulf. And those who stayed but didn't want to go along to get along—well, we all know what happened to them.

I don't know if my generation understood the meaning of what we saw, what we encountered and experienced, but were at a loss about our options, or if we knew exactly where it all was leading but were just sellouts, or if we knew, were at a loss about our options, and so decided to sell out.

I am referring to my own very specific category of failures; those, like me, who cared but chose to do close to nothing. That is, nothing that could possibly involve any sacrifice. Because there is, of course, another category of failure of the heroic variety; those who cared and were actually willing to pay a high price: the disappeared, the dead, the exiles, the political prisoners, the dissidents.

But what's the point of all this? (I have gone over these words twice in red ink in my diary.) Is it that those who, like me, elected to focus on themselves, ended up being the wisest? That the harrowing events since 2011, and the devastation of this generation's aspirations, exonerate my own walkout? That we spent decades repeating to ourselves, "Shame on us, we should be doing something," only to watch, post-2011, our children's anguish, murmuring to ourselves, "Thank God we didn't"? Or, put soberly, had we risen to the challenge when the system was much younger and more susceptible to pressure, would the twenty-first century now be a much kinder place for all of us?

This is where the brush needs to be at its smallest and finest, and the strokes at their most delicate, because I'd like an intact shape to the truth—to my truth. But it seems to me the outlines I have shared are already pretty damning. Or maybe this also is a form of deflection and bluff.

All I can tell you is that anyone who has lived here has lived this.

CHAPTER 4

The Incrementalists

And what about us then? What is left of us? What do we do with the burden of this past? We offer new generations our martyrdom with a tender tear-eyed smile . . ."

—Arwa Salih,
The Stillborn

In this house that has known nothing but a life of struggle, it was foreordained for you to be at war always, constantly striving, aspiring, without respite . . .

Make of your disappointments a thing of wisdom, a call for action . . .

Do not base your happiness on anything that might cause pain to others, for happiness in a despondent and desperate society is utterly worthless.

Your people's well-being is a duty entrusted to you . . . Do not shirk it [no matter the temptation or threat] . . .

—Translated excerpts from my father's letter to
my eight-year-old brother Fadi on June 9, 1967,
on the fourth day of the 1967 War

My father's letter was tucked away for years. In a conversation with Fadi in the early 1980s, Raghida brought it up, and they went rummaging, finding it in a Rowntree Mackintosh box in a cupboard.

By then we had moved houses in Shmeisani, nestling in a cute villa with a small garden one street up from the Civil Defense building. Our fourth home since moving to Jordan in 1962, it was no more than eight minutes away from the first two in Jabal al-Hussein and three streets up from the third, which had a clear view of the old Mukhabarat (Intelligence Service) compound.

Both Shmeisani houses were a stone's throw away from the 3rd Duwwar, at the center of which stood, and still does today, a white concrete cone-like sculpture. On it, column-like, our three loyalties hang in black metal: God, then Homeland, then King.

Raghida, the family's interpreter of dreams and various other-worldly matters, would always say that our second Shmeisani home was inhabited by the kindest of fairies, even kinder than the first one, bestowing upon us the longest run of good luck, good fun, the lushest of gardens, and the most bountiful of fruit trees. The jasmine-filled front porch with the creaking couch swing was for the afternoons; the back garden was for dinners and barbecues. The teeny glassed-in balcony to the side of the far end salon on the ground floor was where we often lounged.

We called it the Bar. It was an enchanted, kitschy little room, with a fuzzy bright green carpet, a 1970s sofa and sister chairs and a beautiful mahogany cabinet from which one could catch the faintest scent of brandy. It's where we went to have breakfast, listen to music, read, think, whisper sweet nothings, and let slip secrets. It's where each morning I would pretend to read the news to my visiting maternal grandmother, Umm Mussbah, making up stories as I went, delivering shockers, like the murder of her beloved Musa al-Sadr, the Lebanese Shiite leader, and cracking up at her mortified reaction; where my visiting maternal grandfather, Hussein (Abu Mussbah), who lived in Africa and whom I barely knew, asked me the day after he arrived in the summer of 1975 if my shorts weren't too short; where, a year later, my mother wept when she was told he had passed away in Beirut; where I wrote my Stanford application when my father left me no choice. It's where I watched him huddle with friends to discuss politics and wished that I were a fly on that wall.

Between the time my father (Abu Fadi) wrote his letter in 1967 and the day Fadi and Raghida found it stood around fifteen years during which time our whole world changed: the monumental victory of Israel; the loss of East Jerusalem and the West Bank (Jordan's "lungs")*; another Palestinian exodus; a Hashemite-PLO feud; an Arab-Israeli war; a Lebanese war; the Camp David Peace Accords between Egypt and Israel; a Persian revolution, a Meccan assault, and an Israeli siege. Much more was going on in the Middle East, but for us, this was the calendar that framed that stretch. The patterns of our existence had taken shape; external turmoil tempered by the good fairies doing their magic in our private realms.

The letter itself is haunting. Four pages long, it telegraphs the toll of a calamitous Arab defeat on a father's heart. It is full of apprehension, the fear that, in a constantly heaving region, his son might just give up and reach for his own salvation and contentment in a universe of one. It's as if he anticipated the impoverishments to come.

My father's words and those of Arwa Salih inform the tenor of the decades that followed '67. His and hers are, with mine, a generational chronicle—a postcolonial one, it has to be said. All the hope initially his, all the despair finally hers: the first rallying

---

*Jordan annexed East Jerusalem and the West Bank in 1950.

cry and the last gasp. And then the stillness—of us. Searing testimonies both that convey the cost exacted by such epic events.

Abu Fadi and Arwa. Two failed revolutionaries who pursued apparently antagonistic paths. My father put his ideological zeal to bed and became a man of the establishment; Arwa furiously owned hers to the end, taking it to her grave, a tormented woman. Both, in their particular youthful journey, felt betrayed. Both exited in adulthood: he to a career of building and trying to change things from within since the other way around had nearly got him killed; she to another country and its cold comforts. It's a very familiar story of disaffection and abandonment. But if there is a thing of beauty about '67, it's the way it illuminates the shared dismay and fury of Arabs whose positions in life would appear to have set them at odds. In this sense, it was the great unifier—that is, before its consequences began to tear us apart.

I didn't know of Arwa and *The Stillborn*, her compiled reflections of that hour, before I began to write *This Arab Life*. It appeared in a book review as if to offer the account of the 1970s generation I was looking for: personal, unvarnished, self-examining. Hers was that extraordinary moment of stunned humiliation in the aftermath of the 1967 "Naksa" that saw popular yearnings erupt and regimes recoil. The last hurrah, as it turned out, when politics and culture dared to let loose their passion and ingenuity. In those heady short years, she was a leader of Egypt's student movement, a Marxist of the die-hard kind.

It's a very painful read, *The Stillborn*, all ferocity and lament about a wrecked generation and its legacy. Of her aspirations and ultimate disappointments, Arwa writes:

> *The demonstrations carried an obscure promise of deliverance, a promise that sank into oblivion under the rubble of a twisted history with no room for inflated dreams. . . . We were a people trying desperately to retrieve its ability to think after a long age of inanity. . . . The generations that came after ours never had the chance to know such vast ambition.*[1]

She failed. Her movement failed. Her generation failed. The entire Arab left failed, she howls, because of its petty ambitions and petite bourgeoisie appetites. For a Marxist, a particularly brutal indictment. The wasteland that this failure helped to usher in would torture her the most. She committed suicide in 1997, in exile in Madrid.

As she predicted, all my generation inherited was her teary-eyed smile.

I have no vivid recollection of June 1967. I only have a faint grasp of shock in the world around me. But I don't remember myself in it. And yet, it felt as if I was nursed on the catastrophe. Such was the impact on people and on land; on sacred cause and sense of self-worth.

I know that during those six days of war we were in Beirut. And, of course, I know that my father stayed behind in Amman. That's it. In fiery times, in a fiery Levant, Lebanon had managed to excuse itself from the regional tumult.

On that June day, when my father wrote the letter to Fadi, he was on an Alitalia flight to the Ivory Coast, exploring another path, another continent, another beginning. He was done, he told himself, and the king, and friends. Done with the Arab world. His disillusionment would last forever, his decision only days. In the end, there were more good reasons to stay than leave—his new passport, new home and career, a baby on the way, gratitude, guilt. How do you walk away from a king who gave you blanket protection against a death warrant issued by your country of birth, and that still hangs over your head? How do you turn your back on him when he asks you to return? When he treats you as a confidant and a friend? These would be his answers to me, whenever '67 came up. And it did—often.

"What choice did I have?" he would ask. And just to add to the bitter sweetness of the past, he and I would muse about how good luck and bad were always at each other's throats in his life, the first somehow always coming from behind and winning. This is how the 1960s started out for him, and how they ended. In 1961, the frantic departures of the political fugitive, by 1972 the soft glow that envelops the blessed.

I chose those few lines from Abu Fadi's letter because they chose me a long time ago. They were the shortest cut to the way he brought us up. They were also the strongest hint that when he was writing the letter, he had not really resolved to leave; that this place had an extraordinary hold on him still. When I shared all this with him recently, he ever so slightly gave me a nod.

Throughout the years, I have often told him that I wish he had left. I said it more for my sake than his. I still say it now, when all, as it were, is memories and dust. But my God, the gall, I often think. To have done and lived so well for so long in the Arab world, and yet to have wanted to be somewhere else, and be someone else. Is it just the exhaustion of belonging to a land that refuses to settle, of pining for a corner of this earth that is more content with itself, less exposed to the elements, less troubled? Or is it the shame? To be the enabler and beneficiary of the very setup you decry as the problem you want to escape. What better resolution of such moral fraudulence than flight!

The dilemmas of the sensitized Arab bourgeoisie, those brawls between narrow interests and high ideals. They're not really much different from, say, Romain Gary's American "moral upper class" in *White Dog*. Except that ours as Arabs are considerably more acute.

To be the witness. The reluctant accomplice. To be in a position of power and know that you are utterly powerless. To be at once privileged and a hair's breadth from being frighteningly defenseless. To regurgitate, like an automaton, the prudence and efficacy of working within the system more to dupe yourself than others. And still with all that, when confronted, to spread your palms, purse your lips, lift your eyebrows, argue helplessness, and go about your business quietly because when it comes down to it, you actually want it all.

We Arabs have a wonderful saying for these love-hate conundrums: *I want it and I spit on it.* Quiescence in exchange for influence, protection, security, opportunity, gain; all the while squirming on the inside every other day. I exaggerate: maybe every few harrowing news flashes or ugly personal encounters, depending on the year's season of deceit and discontent. All the same, the retreats and giveaways are daily, constant, almost subliminal. They typically start very early and come in trickles, easing the indignity of what ends up being surrender on the grandest of scales: the political activism you ditch forever because you're playing with fire in a country of martial law; the rare public criticism you stifle with so much weaseling, it barely stumbles out of your mouth; the repertoire of physical gestures tailored for public view that allows you to really express yourself without ever really expressing yourself; code words over the telephone, winks and smirks, feet that surreptitiously nudge other feet under the dinner table when a sensitive topic is broached.

And if you doubted this was all necessary, every so often, those good gentlemen tapping your phone, for your own safety of course, might in passing remind you that they were keeping watch. As the spy chief joked to my father once in the 1970s: "So, Umm Fadi isn't too happy with the vegetables the grocery man is sending her these days, huh?" Just so went the gentle tut-tutting when my father was advised a few years later that Fadi's political activism in Washington, DC, where he was studying for his BA degree, should be dialed down a notch or two—or three. They didn't spell out the objections. They didn't have to: loyalty, Palestine, and politics. The last two, we all knew, cancelled out the first. You could cry forever with abandon for Palestine, but you could not on your own, and unprompted, rally or demonstrate in its name, or any other name, for that matter.

We didn't think much about the advice. We didn't have to. As children of privilege, we had long before learned the rules and the permitted wriggle room, the terms and conditions. It was a rather tight arrangement in a hierarchy cobbled together from society's different cliques and classes, each specifically designed to make the pact eternal—a catholic union of a sort until we're all six feet under. Coercion was ever-present, of course, on some occasions very coy, on others brazen. The mere specter of it, for many of us, was enough to do away with all temptations. The idea was, therefore, to push our luck up to the boundary of reproofs. King Hussein didn't much indulge contrarian opinions, but he positively shimmered with good will and mercy in comparison with his fellow travelers in the region. And if you happened to know and like him, which I did even if my political inclinations were quarrelsome, the gratitude was all the more instinctive. So, we reflexively compared and contrasted, appreciated the big-heartedness, and proceeded to play by the rules.

You grow up learning the twists and turns, the ins and outs, the strength of this bond, much like you subconsciously soak up your name, your religion, your mother's temperament, your father's habits. By the time you can walk straight and talk in full sentences, you've already absorbed who and what you are. And when you've fully outgrown your puppy love, made peace with your acne, received your high school diploma, and kissed your parents goodbye before heading for university in Beirut or London or the US, you are ready—if that's your thing—to use up every inch of that wriggle room. In oppressive settings, this is how the human spirit tends to endure. Ours certainly did, although the skeptics may dismiss this as little more than the self-serving vindication of a silent generation, or worse, of complicit upper-class mutts.

When we all readied ourselves to go to university, there developed a tradition among us West Ammanis that very quickly turned into a ritual. The evening before takeoff, a legion of us would descend upon the departing friend's home and launch into a revelry of adieus. Lovers would swoon and cuddle, friends would be in tears, hugging each other. Chatter, laughter, and lights would animate Amman's otherwise torpid neighborhoods. Girls and boys, we would prance our way toward the hour of departure, hesitantly looking back. One by one, we would scatter at the end of every August to our chosen foreign cities.

I don't know how and why this ritual came to be. It wasn't so with my sister Raghida and her age group, a mere few years ahead of us. The way she tells it, they all couldn't wait to get out. Hers was a time of inane parties, timid boyfriends, silly giggles and stolen, clumsy kisses, endless mother-daughter quibbles about skirt length and that constant parental refrain: no, you can't. Ours were the late nights, the hot kisses behind the diving pool of the Sports City, devil-may-care vacations on Aqaba's shores, parental white flags of surrender over a sea of bikinis.

How quickly attitudes change! By the mid-1970s, Jordan's civil feud was tentatively settling into an ugly memory. You could almost hear the monarchy's sigh of relief. The city was more at ease, more confident—at peace. At least that was the view from where we were living, the vistas we were meant to see, a false reprieve, while the very mode of life in Jordan was being dismantled piece by piece. Perhaps such was our intuitive awareness of the vastness of the moment to come, of the impermanence of now, the sense that all would not, could not, ever be the same again, that those farewell parties were our rite of passage into a world more real.

Because these were also the years of the purge, when Palestinians, especially those with a leftist pedigree, were eased out of the bureaucracy. The same years that saw the Muslim Brotherhood reap the rewards of standing by their king during his battle with the PLO. When the MB's Ishaq al-Farhan became president of Jordan University and turned it from a benign campus where male and female students would share desks and benches and sandwiches, into a hub of Islamist ferment. Those same years when the veil began to frame many a woman's face and the beard became a statement; when the business of intelligence and politics began to mix more openly.

It was also when the Sports City, in what seemed like the blink of an eye, changed from the harbinger of good tidings to an omen of bad ones. You couldn't put your finger on it. Folktale-like, a wonderland, incandescent and happy, turned on a dime and grew dark, sour, and grim. "We went that first year to the US, came back, and el-Madineh was another country," as Fadi had neatly summed it up once. It was one of the clues we were picking up at the door to the '80s that this was a season of migration to another narrative entirely: messier, more garish, smaller. More fences were going up; we were sticking more and more to our own turf, class, kith, and kin. Every summer of return, another piece of us, and the city we knew, had disappeared or was fading.

Eight idyllic years we had: 1972–1980. That was it. Eight years at the movies. After that, we couldn't be oblivious to the trends even if they meant nothing to us at first sight.

I'd like to blame my generation's dull reaction on our immaturity—we were barely in our twenties when it all began to go south. But our once riotous older siblings didn't budge either. I think the implications simply did not sink deep enough into us. The mutations happened as if haphazardly, some coming with swirling rumors that they were temporary or exaggerated or unfortunate, soon-to-be corrected errors of judgment. They washed over us in small waves. We still had our breezy neighborhoods, Romero or Leonardo da Vinci for restaurants, piccata al limone and J&B on the rocks for quiet nights, the Intercontinental or Holiday Inn discos for loud ones, Cezar for Arabic groove, the Jordan Valley or Nabataean Petra for the weekends, Roman Jerash for Friday lunches. Amman still felt quaint, cozy, clean, secure. Crime was something practically unheard of, and so were traffic jams. War was raging in Beirut; Damascus was not exactly tempting, neither was Saddam's Baghdad. The Gulf was even more of a desert and Sadat's Cairo didn't seem to have any edge over our city. What did it matter if we West Ammani girls, with our bikinis, did not feel welcome anymore in el-Madineh? The Holiday Inn or Intercontinental pools would do. And wasn't Ishaq al-Farhan a bit of a wet blanket? And didn't the king detest wet blankets? Wasn't he modern? A moderate? In control? Doing his usual delicate balancing act? And who wanted to head downtown anyhow? Indian movies were passé, Egyptian cinema too. Older movie stars like Ahmad Mazhar and Magda were barely hanging by a thread. Now, only for icons like Adel Imam, Souad Hosny, Faten Hamamah, and Yusra were excursions made to the other side. Then VHS film cassettes came to the rescue and helped us dump practically the entire issue in technology's lap.

Besides, there was college and escape. For many of Amman's middle class, Jordan and Yarmuk universities, perhaps too new, or local, weren't the destination of choice. It wasn't so for Lebanese, who had the American University of Beirut (AUB), L'Université Saint Joseph (USJ), and Beirut University College (BUC) for their undergraduate years, or for Syrians, Iraqis, and Egyptians who also opted for local institutions.

Weekends in the Jordan Valley, early 1980s.

Jerash, early 1980s.

Our academic sojourn in the US was a wonderful taste of un-encumbered aliveness. We were essentially free. We were now individuals, anonymous, decision makers, explorers, if that was what we wanted. And many of us did. We were strangers and in its be-and-let-be ease America was so welcoming. We just drank in the culture, imbibed its quirks, learned its slang. In no time at all, most of us cruised along pretty much like our American friends. My own early start at Maryland's Holton Arms School was a leg up on the rest of my Jordanian group. I had to leave for the US when I finished the tenth grade to accompany my moth-er and my sister Iman, who, at the age of nine, was diagnosed with severe hearing loss and learning disabilities.

My parents decided to enroll her in the Children's Nation-al Hospital's rehabilitation program to help her catch up to the greatest degree possible. Fadi had just been accepted at George Washington University, Raghida was finishing her senior year at Santa Clara University in California, and Asma was married with two kids in Beirut. Off you go, my father said.

I adjusted quickly, struggling only at first with my surprising-ly weak English and my friends' tendency to call me Amaol or Ammel. It's at Holton where I first learned how to tango with America. It's where I met my lifelong best friend Joye, one class ahead of me, who plonked herself down next to me one day during my free period and asked, "Where are you from?" It's where I met my first Jewish acquaintances and friends, a few avid supporters of Israel, others not. Holton is where I had my early training in debates. It's where my love of American poli-tics developed under the remarkable Mrs. Cole, my American history teacher; where I fell for philosophy because of the bril-liant and wonderfully eccentric Mrs. Smink, who gave me an A+ on my imagined dialogue between Plato and Machiavelli. That wonderful American high school is where I learned how to dream as fluently in English as I did in Arabic; to ask for help when I needed it, to second-guess myself.

In all this, I know I was very fortunate. The absence of prejudice, the openness with which I was received, the healthy curiosity about habits and origins. Holton may well have been in its own special cocoon, but the story was essentially the same at Georgetown. Pure luck, I have to assume. During the hostage crisis in Iran in 1979, Fadi and some Arab male friends were often heckled and taunted with, "Iranian, go home." There were furious arguments and reactions on many a campus, of course. Where we all felt the loneliest was concerning Palestine. It became an education all by itself. In the old country passions lay low; in America they soared. Amman was an echo chamber; the US was a shouting match. Back home, the Palestinian cause reigned as queen, its history an immaculate gown, its justness a glittering crown, its purity the Virgin Mary's. In America, it was an out-of-towner, a stranger, a loser, unwelcome and friendless. In newspapers, on television, in the movies, in Congress, at the White House, on campus, the gown was Israel's—and certainly the crown. We had to hit the books, know the facts, learn verbal fencing, and appreciate, even admire, the skills and convictions of the adversary.

In America, our world was turned upside down. Overnight, a hallowed truth morphed into an argument. We could not just love Palestine; we had to get to know it. And who could have tutored us better than Edward Said, I. F. Stone, Alfred Lilienthal, Hannah Arendt, Henry Cattan, and Noam Chomsky? *The Question of Palestine, The Zionist Connection, Palestine and International Law,* and later *The Fateful Triangle* became our bibles. We studied the different strands of Zionism and the tensions between them; we were captivated by the writings of Jewish philosophers and thinkers like Martin Buber and Ahad Ha'am; their warnings about the dangers of political Zionism and their advocacy for the spiritual and cultural motif in "Jewish return" to Palestine. We took courses on the Arab-Israeli conflict, went to seminars, speeches, conferences. We joined rallies, many of us squirming at some of the chants, just as many sniggering at others: *no, no to Sadat, yes, yes, to Gamal! No, no to Sadat, yes, yes, Arafat! Today Zimbabwe, Tomorrow Palestine!* We screamed our hearts out for Palestine.

In America, we learned that sacred cows graze everywhere in the land of the free just as they do in the land of the oppressed, and that among them, Israel was the most sacred cow of all.

We learned that there was something to Hegel's words: "Genuine tragedies in the world are not conflicts between right and wrong. They are conflicts between two rights." Indeed, Israel's defenders were as convinced of their case as we were of ours. And in this clash of narratives, we had no claim on America's heart or imagination. In fact, we didn't have a chance in hell.

In America, we grew up.

We understood that we were always being watched by the good folks back home and understood the general rule too: that if you didn't take matters too far, organize too much, blabber too loudly, you could, more or less, get away with it. But if you took your politics too seriously and dared branch out, you very soon got used to paying a visit to the old Mukhabarat building in Abdali on your way in and out of Amman, earning a spot in that file cabinet and a regular seat in that proverbial waiting room.

For my part, I spent four years at Georgetown University's Foreign Service School entanglement free. My apparent reserve was peculiar for a major in international politics, I admit. But I was just not interested in the menu on offer—not in the PLO vs. the Palestinian Front for the Liberation of Palestine (PFLP) vs. the Palestinian Democratic Front for the Liberation of Palestine (PDFLP). Not in the Syrian Social Nationalist Party (SSNP) vs. the Nasserites vs. the Iraqi Ba'ath vs. the Syrian Ba'ath vs. the Maoists vs. the communists vs. the socialists vs. the Muslim Brotherhood. Not in late-night, smoke-filled meetings, and campus fights. Not in Hussein vs. Arafat vs. Assad vs. Gaddafi vs. Saddam vs. Sadat. It was an Arab arena in miniature, so to every party, ideology, organization, manifesto, slogan, invitation, I gave the yawn. I lent an ear only to Edward Said, Ibrahim Abu-Lughod, and company. I immersed myself in existentialism because such was and remains my view of the meaning of me in this bizarre universe. I fell in love with Albert Camus because I fell in love with *The Plague*, *The Stranger*, and the French-Algerian conflicts within him; because I fell in love with his magnificent black-and-white photographs, trench coat, cigarettes and all.

❖ ❖ ❖ ❖

When we came back to Amman for good by the mid-1980s, we quickly fell into the usual morphine-like torpor, that wonderful quietude of the mind. We couldn't help it. Politics, the state made clear, was forbidden territory, the cityscape was still so easy on the eye, the go-to places a handful, the radius of your daily routine 15 minutes in any direction, the scope of it one notch above tiny. The 1st, 2nd, and 3rd Duwwar were still favorite afternoon rides. Culture was art exhibitions at the Alia Gallery; books and magazines at the Book Corner on the 1st Duwwar, with bespectacled Uncle Bassel always receiving us with a smile. Theater was practically nonexistent, and so were literary ateliers. The press was strictly the state's even when it wasn't, and there were just two television channels. The chattering classes may have felt denied, but they did what they do best: chatter about it in their living rooms among family and close friends.

Our own small group, like many others, no doubt, found much nourishment among ourselves; in the friendship of Ali al-Jabri, a tour de force in Arab art; in fortuitous encounters and friendships with wonderful visitors, like Iraqi artists Essam al-Said and Nuha al-Radi, Palestinian scholar Ibrahim Abu-Lughod, journalist Christopher Dickey. We would huddle on the weekends, over lunches and dinners, chatting away for hours.

Not much intruded on this picture in my own one-year stint as a political reporter for the *Jerusalem Star* right after graduation in 1983. But I saw enough to know that something about the place was different. Big villas with outlandish designs started going up in West Amman, many of them engraved with *hatha min fadli rabbi* (this is by the favor of my Lord) above the main door. Women wearing burqas driving their Mercedes-Benzes were being spotted across town. The effects of the oil boom of the '70s had begun to display themselves fully. Droves of skilled hands from Jordan, Egypt, Syria, and Sudan went to work in ministries, schools, institutions, and companies in the Gulf. Remittances flooded back. Consumption jumped. Habits changed. Islamism with a Wahhabi twist started to spread.

The reporting I did for the *Jerusalem Star* took me to people, places, and issues that were already more or less known to me.

Jerusalem Star interview, from left: Fadia Faqih; interview subject, François Larché; Sanaa Aloul; and author circa 1984.

If you cared two bits, you knew that Amman's languor belied undercurrents that were less than sanguine. I was one of those who cared two bits and so I knew. Not that I knew what to do about it, or even thought that I could—beyond, that is, sounding off with friends that things were not right in the government, in the refugee camps, in the countryside, on the east side of Amman. For us on the west side, it was as if we were suspended at midpoint between make-believe and reality. There were no thick screens or hard barricades. With such short distances between estranged geographies, you couldn't avoid contact or scrub out the panoramas of distress from your workdays. But hardly anything seemed of any immediate consequence to us personally, so we just observed and, when particularly moved, filed the memory away and muttered under our breath.

We, native voyeurs, each have a locked chest in the darkest and farthest corner of our psyche, swarming with visuals, utterly fleeting and yet immortal. Put together they're like a photo album, each snapshot reminding us of a premonition or a missed opportunity or a foreboding; each forever the emblem of a moment that was to evolve into one infinitely less hopeful.

Every time I dust off the early '80s—the way we were, the things we saw, the clues we had about what awaited us all—I find myself back in Tafileh, a small town in southern Jordan, chatting with an old gentleman at one of the town's campaign headquarters for the 1984 parliamentary by-election. He was about seventy or so, with a trimmed white beard that matched the sparkling white *hatta w 'igal* which graced his gray, belted *thawb*. Fadia, a fellow reporter at the *Jerusalem Star*, and I were mingling in one of the busy campaign offices, asking questions of the men to get a feel for what really counted in the vote. They kept insisting that tribal loyalties and family connections played no part in their choice. The farce went on and on, as they continued to fib and I continued to press in the hope of a good quote. And then, tired of the back and forth, this old man finally put us all out of our misery. He turned to me and said in his local vernacular, "Ya ukht (sister), you want it to be Swayssra (Switzerland)? It will never be Swayssra."

He was looking at me when he brought the discussion to a halt. I don't know why the old man chose Switzerland, of all Western countries, as his ideal. Perhaps our close encounters with England and the US had left him unimpressed with their example. At any rate, it certainly was not my fantasies that he was after. I had none. It was the entire sham in which we all, eyes wide open, were playing our part. We laughed out loud, fibbers and notetakers alike, and then carried on: they with the trappings of faux democracy, Fadia and I with the pretense that we were actually covering an event that implied something more than nothing. How badly we were already doing then, how well we knew it, and still, how desperately 2019, as I write these lines, pales before the shine of 1984. Not only for us.

"And while we were falling in love and singing and dreaming," reminisced Syrian writer Wael Sawah recently about his Damascene days in the 1970s:

> . . . *little by little, the street was turning more Islamist, our sisters veiling, even as our mothers stayed unveiled. Little by little, social ruptures were deepening, and little by little our relationship with the people was growing more frail. Syrians went to Saudi*

Arabia, came back wearing the dishdasha, behind them women in burqas. And then started the trend of religious classes in schools and houses. Little by little, with a nod from the regime of Hafez Assad, the Islamists spread their tentacles slowly but steadily into every aspect of cultural and social life.[2]

Much draws us apart, Wael and I. He was an active member of the Syrian Labor Communist Party and went to prison. Ideology never meant much to me, political parties even less. He let go of his writing for politics and lived to regret it; I never let go of any passion for the sake of politics, but I did sacrifice politics, a passion, for the lightness of being. He is from a family that has devoted itself to cultural and political activism. In the same way that Abu Fadi fled from Lebanon to Jordan for safety, Wael's father escaped the Syrian Ba'ath in 1963 for Lebanon. But we are a brood whose father abandoned his political subversiveness in 1962, at the borders of Jordan. Our love of culture was experienced through books, fiery discussions behind closed doors, and friendships with artists, writers, and poets who graced our world mostly through Raghida, the artist of the house. There is also the age: Wael's prime was in the '70s, mine a decade later. And yet, as I read his serialized memoirs on *Daraj*, a digital news site, I find myself fascinated by the similarities: the same undertows across countries, the same alienations and abdications. And now, almost the same flashbacks by generations scavenging for answers in that chest of regrets and remembrances.

The rest of the century, for us, took its cue from this mood and tempo. Every year, every month, Jordan, a "lower middle-income country," copes with internal misfires and external shocks. The International Monetary Fund (IMF) comes to town in 1989. Riots start in dirt poor Ma'an in the south as fuel and food prices rise. The government resigns. Parliamentary elections are held to help people vent. The Muslim Brotherhood gains even more ground. Trouble erupts between the Gulf, the West, and King

Hussein, who refuses to side against Saddam in the Gulf War of 1991. Around 350,000 refugees join us in the city; well-off Palestinians from Kuwait in this batch. The capital grows without much of a plan. A chaos of new streets, new business centers, high rises, and villas.

After that, we frankly lost count. Atrophy set in practically everywhere through ineptitude or negligence or good intentions gone rogue. King Hussein dies in 1999; Prince Abdullah, his eldest, ascends. America invades Iraq in 2003, producing new refugees: hundreds of thousands of Iraqis this time around. Foreign debt balloons. A state, barely sixty years old, is all but out of breath. Successive governments were simply all out of ideas: in education, in the shrinking social safety nets, in the water shortages, in the breakneck speed urban sprawl, in the poverty index that refuses to come down and employment figures that refuse to go up, in the highways and tunnels that crisscross a bloated capital, severing continuities and decapitating memory . . . It's as if the state, whacked every which way and overwhelmed, had decided to cut and paste its way into the future.

Then suddenly we were all middle-aged!

Where exactly were my friends and I in all this? We took long, lingering looks from the windows of our bubbles at changing streets and norms, changing dress codes and textbooks, changing cities and landscapes, and knew that all would not be well.

But what to do? What else, but fall in love and sing and dream. We did a lot of that. We built careers and families. We read, partied, traveled, packed, and left, mainly to the Gulf and a rising United Arab Emirates (UAE). I ended up in London. By 1988, I was an executive in Aramex, Fadi's global logistics company and in Beirut by 1991. We had money, education, skills, opportunity. So, it was more or less business as usual ('adi, as we say). Nothing seemed particularly traumatic to me. To the region—yes, to the country—absolutely. To me, not exactly. Like so many in my tribe, I internalized, adapted, and kept walking, comfortable in insulation layers deep.

Were we playing psychological tricks on ourselves? Plausible, certainly for our Lebanese friends in war-ravaged Beirut trying to carry on with normal routines in a life that was anything but normal. But I am not so sure. The likelier truth is that we just cruised along, adjusting every now and then to the cadence of the chaos. If we had a love for the extracurricular or an urge to venture out of our comfort zones, we "civically engaged," as it now is described. And this was long before that expression and its asinine sister, "empowerment," were put to hard labor by nongovernmental organizations (NGOs) everywhere, eventually turning both into spent, over-the-hill clichés.

We engaged because it was permitted and, therefore, safe. Because there was nowhere else to go to add zest and weight to our existence except this sphere conveniently called "civil society." Because the divides were becoming increasingly glaring and the state's inadequacies more so still. Because it was sexy. Because we bought the line that our work would be transformational. . . .

I could go on and on listing motivations; they were countless and we were many. Our ages ranged between twenty-one and thirty, our family income between high and extremely high. We were casually liberal, secular, or not religiously inclined. To be sure, among us were those with a sharper edge, a leftist streak, a deeper commitment, a somewhat more rebellious spirit, but this was all wrapped in intentions so convincingly banal they escaped detection.

Some of us established sports clubs on the side. Others contributed to or patronized charities with all sorts of acronyms offering any combination of BKB: bread, kerosene, and blankets. Still others worked with or donated to NGOs for cultural revival, income generation, women's "empowerment," artistic expression, poverty alleviation, children's rights, women's rights, legal aid . . . You name it, we offered it. Into practically every vacuum created by our inept and callous governments, we stepped in with considerable resources or bandages and balms. We did so not as organized groups, but as human beings who happened to have common decency, or a passion, or a concern, or a misguided sense of purpose, or pretentious *noblesse oblige*. We had no vision or strategy, working haphazardly and apart, keeping to our lacunae, grottos, and friends.

Over time, we settled so well into our "public spiritedness," that the generation of the '90s was inspired to do the same, but in much larger numbers. The region buzzed with every imaginable NGO championing every imaginable cause, some serious, diligent, and focused, many ridiculous and clueless, tripping all over each other in an overcrowded, freewheeling, fragmented, untidy universe. A do-good frenzy. By the end of the century, we were hearing about the supposed rise of Arab civil society, as if it were a juggernaut of genuine, sweeping reforms. No fewer than 15,000 organizations jostled for space in Egypt in the '90s. They topped 30,000 in 2008.[3] In Jordan, a mere fifty civil society organizations (CSOs) operated in 1966; by 2008, they had grown to 1,500.[4] Seven years later, upward of 4,200 associations had "around 1.5 million members in total, equivalent to 43 percent of the working-age population of more than 3.5 million people."[5]

While some of these are now giant organizations, others have remained niche. Some have done very meaningful work, others have become specialist fundraisers vomiting jargon and spinning yarns. Some have—knowingly and not—peddled foreign-driven agendas or pushed local ones, others have been stubbornly grassroots. But for all the hype, the overwhelming majority has actually stuck to the basics: humanitarian assistance and charity.[6] This, while an increasingly miserly state has looked on, very carefully nodding, probably even giggling on occasion, always watching and, should we stray into forbidden space, finger-wagging us back into line.

If the state's apparent indulgence was a boon for us civic "chumps," as claimed by our critics, it was a bonanza for Islamists of every stripe. In almost every locale, they dominated the nonprofit map with a whole range of interventions, from bread all the way to orphanages, schools, and universities. We did our bit, they did "God's work." We came with numerous motives, they came with one. We were professedly apolitical, they were screamingly ideological. We were all over the place, they stuck together and to their faith. Since those initial years, little has changed. In entire districts, over vast territories, they were (and remain) the only presence on the ground.

I tiptoed into this scene when I was twenty-three. "NGOism" was about to become the latest craze. In my third year of work between my bachelor's and my master's, I became a social worker and project manager at Nour al-Hussein Foundation, a newly minted royal NGO. The experience helped. I stayed away from the field, surmising that my contrarian character would soon enough get me into trouble.

It was two decades later that I began devoting time to Ruwwad, a community-based initiative that Fadi had just launched in Jabal al-Natheef, one of East Amman's severely marginalized Palestinian quasi-camps. He was then still CEO of Aramex. By 2003, I had decided to leave a corporate career and focus more on writing and other interests. I also wanted to have a closer relationship with Jordan. I had been away for too long and I needed to get to know it again, even though I had built a life in Beirut. Ruwwad would allow conversations, camaraderie, and collaborations that would have been very difficult for me to forge otherwise in my old home. It had an organic presence in the locales where it worked, and it was a grassroots organization free from political bartering, which was rather unusual in disenfranchised communities where transactional, service-based relationships are the rule. For me, it was the ideal re-entry into the Amman I wanted to get to know better.

Ruwwad has at its heart the offer of a college scholarship in exchange for volunteerism. Qualifying youth of the surrounding neighborhoods get a scholarship and volunteer in areas that are of interest to them at the center. At all the Ruwwads, and there are now six, there is also space for our scholars, males and females, to come together every Saturday morning, as part of their volunteerism, and explore issues that concern them. Ruwwad is not ours alone. Wherever we are, we have established it in partnership with a small group of like-minded private individuals and companies who fund the endeavor annually and provide other types of support, from advocacy with the state, to legal aid, internships, training, health, and sports programs. There are now Ruwwads in Jordan, Lebanon, Egypt, and the West Bank.

❖ ❖ ❖ ❖

You can write poetry about what neoliberalism does to the human condition, but you can't throw the label into most conversations without drawing a blank. In Arabic, it rings almost like a tongue twister: al-neyyoliberaliyyah. You sound pedantic and pompous just uttering the term. Not the case, say, with authoritarianism, political Islam, or capitalism. All deeply experienced, and all very recognizable, although the general population may be a little fuzzy on the details.

"NGOism" fares no better than its parent. I have rarely heard or seen it used outside of academia. I have never come across an Arabic equivalent either. And yet, this pair, this mother and child, have flourished over the past forty years in much of the Arab world, touching our lives in profound ways.

The gist of neoliberalism is actually rather simple. It instructs the state to scrimp and save: slash basic subsidies, shrink social safety nets, privatize public services, drop trade protections, dismantle regulations, raise taxes, and reduce the public payroll. There is no better way to balance a budget and unleash an economy's true potential, it argues. Its tagline is: Don't Be Timid, Be Bold! To the individual, especially the one at the bottom of the pyramid, neoliberalism says you're largely on your own, as you should be. So, pull yourself up by your bootstraps and find your way in that wonderfully free and competitive market of all things.

We can credit the IMF with spreading this Western innovation anywhere it came to the "rescue" in the developing world. But even before it was all the rage in the 1980s, President Augusto Pinochet of Chile had adopted it in the mid-1970s, soon after he dispatched Marxist President Salvador Allende.

"NGOism" took hold, largely because neoliberalism took off. In countries with robust dictatorial instincts, where repression of organized resistance is routine, you couldn't hope for a better alternative to popular defiance than civil society's NGOs. The state got its fleet of harmless humanitarians, the humanitarians got their safe activism, and the West got its supposed gradual reforms that assured a "peaceful and stable" order. The strugglers, meanwhile, got their self-help programs, all designed to ease the suffering and/or equip them as full-fledged members of this brave new world.

Much has been written about what we, the moral or complicit or confused Arab bourgeoisies, have presumably accomplished by helping soften the state's blows, or the damage we supposedly wrought by softening them through our NGOs. On the less forgiving side of the scale, to quite a few leftist cognoscente, we were (and still are) a foolish, boisterous gang blithely making noise and playing house on the killing fields. Dupes, or worse, performing our assigned tasks of dulling pain and diluting anger.

For proof, look around you, they say. After forty years of hyperactive charity and philanthropy and civic engagement and empowerment and rights' advocacy and social services, ask yourself in which country are marginalized communities less so now than they were then? Which public education system is producing better students now than then? Which judiciary has become more independent and just? Which rural terrains have become less parched? Which public health sector takes better care of the destitute and infirm? Where have the poor become less poor, the middle class more secure, the rich more accountable? What regime, pre- or post-2011, beat a genuine and lasting political, economic, social, or environmental retreat because of us civic warriors?

None, obviously. But how well had the "revolutionaries" done in their own heyday? Isn't that the essence of our predicament as pragmatists? Their "revolutionary" failure. How many of us NGOers, in the first place, came out of our hideouts to consciously make a sweeping difference? In this golden period of "NGOization," which had carried us from youthful exuberance to adult sobriety, we simply mobilized to nudge the law, improve the odds in various areas of need and urgency; in this neighborhood and that village, of this family and that street, in this new shanty town and that age-old slum. No more, no less.

For critics, it might well be that all this has been little more than a theater of pretense. By sponsoring civil society organizations, the West has pretended to support genuine economic and political reforms, and by tolerating such endeavors, our regimes have feigned an embrace of the same. As for the rest of us, I can't imagine what in the daily grind of picking away at monumental hardships would have led any of us, except the idiots and dilettantes, to believe that we were heroic game changers rather than hard-nosed opportunists.

The truth is that this is the only space that has been made available by notoriously prickly and cynical states, and we have readily accepted the wriggle room. Viewed one way, this is a portrait of generational capitulation. Viewed another, it's an extraordinary generational exercise in incremental activism. Of course, nothing stands in the way of a lens that pulls in both angles. For how could there have ever been such a collective embrace of the piecemeal had there not been such pervasive oppression and such wholesale submission to it?

Nothing stands in the way of an ever-evolving picture either. After the 2011 revolts, our rulers have, in fact, found themselves as impatient with us as they are with almost everyone else. At the mention of rights—human, civil, religious, digital, gay, women's, worker's, farmer's—the axe falls, organizations are shuttered, accounts are frozen, and people are branded or imprisoned as foreign stooges, or terrorists, or hooligans, or morality polluters. The situation acquires a tragicomic quality when organizations, unable to raise any private local funding for fear of the authorities' wrath, have to rely on Western support, which makes them, in turn, more vulnerable to attack as tools of Western conspiracies, not only by states themselves often beholden to the West, but by malcontents whose wooden habit is to see foreign intrigue behind every NGO.

Is this even a halfway decent description of us in this epoch of pragmatism? An elite demobilized by the conniving duo of despotism and neoliberalism. Is that it, more or less? What deterrent, after all, is more effective than tyranny to human aspiration? At once capricious and constant, blunt and crafty, sweeping and personal, tyranny can make a genuine dunce out of you. A collaborator. A coward. A cheat. A con artist. Without you ever meaning or wanting to. It did so to most of us. It does so every day still, from the dread of the prison cell and other such terrors, to the daily negotiations with the Kafkaesque, and the lies and bribes you fork out to buy short cuts, peace of mind, or "friends." You can get very lazy living under its spell, this tyranny. Incurious, glib even. Because it is so potent, it has that remarkable capacity to render you innocent of all blame. You are, with total justification, a victim, and victims never have to explain themselves.

But I am compelled to ask: are despotism and its friend, neoliberalism, explanation enough? Is it even reasonable to disentangle the heap of motivations that induced quiet in an entire generation, an entire class? By me? Here? From a quest so very personal?

This hasn't been an easy chapter to write. I would have liked to be more intimate, uninhibited by sentiments that want to deny and protect. But, frankly, this is the best I can do—for now. Prying open the self for strangers to look in is bound to start with the smaller windows. And what is this book if not a collection of dormers and skylights? Still, I wonder if I have at least managed to offer a sense of the times as we came of political age in the '80s. If I have clearly depicted our collective response to a shared predicament, even though we were riven by the usual divides: borders, income levels, religion, gender, politics. The pragmatism that became our *modus vivendi* in a politically barren Arab world; the loneliness that ironically conquered ever more space in societies perennially cuddled by family, religion, and community; the silos that mushroomed everywhere as a result. The human spirit that continued to pulse, but now restrained—here reactive and timid, there creative but sly. Whatever our person, that was our journey—caravans of the disinherited and the disaffected.

I wonder as I hope!

In doing so, I bow to human identity's refusal to be pinned down, its tendency to be a fluid composition of contradictions and inconsistencies, of elasticities that render it much more resistant to labeling than we care to admit. I bow also to the primacy of context in shaping motive and choice. In a terribly coercive climate, how does one define freedom of choice? Self-interest? Agency? Not philosophically, not in the abstract, not according to this school of thought or that, but day-to-day, Monday to Sunday, dawn to dusk?

I run these questions across every aspect of Arab life on every occasion when I am about to pronounce judgment on something or someone. I don't often have an easy answer, but I never walk into a conversation without them.

Arwa wrote in *The Stillborn* of the bourgeoisie, "This is the class that always claims to speak in the name of the people even when it is bent on betraying them."[7] Spoken like a true Marxist. And I am comfortable with it. I would even say that *This Arab Life* is its own argument of the same. But then, aren't we all traitors in the Arab world? In that most human sense, I mean. The only kind that counts in the end.

CHAPTER 5

Uncle George and Comrade Michel

When you think about it, when you think about Jew and Palestinian not separately, but as part of a symphony, there is something magnificently imposing about it. A very rich, also very tragic, also in many ways desperate history of extremes—opposites in the Hegelian sense—that is yet to receive its due.

—Edward Said

In the post-1967 hysteria, Arabhood itself wailed, tore its hair, and slapped its face in anguish and regret. Nizar Qabbani, the legendary crooner of Arabic love poetry, pleaded with my generation in "Footnotes to the Book of the Setback."

Arab children,
Corn ears of the future,
You will break our chains.
Kill the opium in our heads,
Kill the illusions.
Arab children,
Don't read about our suffocated generation,
We are a hopeless case,
As worthless as a water-melon rind.
Don't read about us,
Don't ape us,
Don't accept us,
Don't accept our ideas,
We are a nation of crooks and jugglers.
Arab children,
Spring rain,
Corn ears of the future,
You are the generation that will overcome defeat.

We did not overcome. We didn't even try. When we came of age, we just looked back, surveyed the panoramic ruins, concluded that, after all that was said and done, it had all been for naught. We looked around us for new inspiration, and saw none; we looked ahead and did ourselves the biggest favor. We acted on the most urgent of Qabbani's pleadings and killed all the illusions.

Not a single regime toppled because of '67. Remember! Not one. Not Nasser's in Egypt. Not the Ba'ath in Syria.* Not the monarchy in Jordan. Practically every slogan and conviction and dream fell with the fallen soldiers. But none of the regimes. We took the hint. If the earthquake of '67 shook heaven and earth but did not bring down a single one of them, who were we to set the land free? If the furious generation of the '70s, with its socialists, Marxists, and nationalists organizing strikes and sit-ins and riots, could not seize the moment after '67, why would we, the generation of the '80s, succeed where they had failed?

Through every precarious moment in the 1970s the Arab order held. Remember! We just kept chugging along through hiccups and seizures. Hope went numb and passion went to sleep. All lights were kept terribly dim except for those illuminating our mosques. (With the state's consent, remember.) So, bar Palestine, the calling before which even the worst of Arab enemies rhetorically kneeled, adulthood for my generation was strangely free from any compelling sentiment or idea—that is, unless you had an attachment to your prayer rug and worry beads.

When scholars dub the decade of my bloom as the dawn of the Neoliberal Age, I nod, but I wonder all the same because of the tiniest of caveats. I would be happy, of course, to blame our stupor on neoliberalism and its assortment of gizmos that presumably lulled us into joining the conspiracy. But in all honesty, as it approached, we were already pretty much subdued and primed for the kill. There were no social movements courting my generation before neoliberalism appeared on our shores, no political parties or trade unions coaching us on our interests and rights, no martyred Allendes to mourn. The truth is there

---

*The Arab Socialist Ba'ath Party came to power in Syria in 1963. In 1967, Nurreddine al-Atassi was president of the Syrian Republic, but Salah Jadid was the actual power behind the presidency. Hafez Assad ousted him in 1970.

was not much resistance among us Arabs, certainly not from my generation, for neoliberalism to commandeer. By the time it appeared on the scene, the architecture of dissent had been all but dismantled.

But I am not playing favorites here, the way social scientists must. I am not particularly concerned with which motivations outpaced others in my generation's disdain for politics. Nor do I pretend to be able to describe the many nuances that color our pragmatism and submissiveness. My quest, as I confessed a few pages ago, is actually more intimate in purpose, much closer to my heart. In interrogating my past to fathom this sense of resignation, do I content myself with identifying tyranny and neoliberalism as my generation's twin evils? First breaking us through fear, then teaching us how to dull the agony? Was my generation's submissiveness purely the work of despots in cahoots with foreign meddlers? Or are we at least partly complicit in our own silence?

Defeat has special resonance for any people, but for us Arabs, it is a burden like no other. Because of our manifold defeats, we think of ourselves as broken and put upon. In 1920, we were forcibly denied any say in our future, as victorious Britain and France proceeded to divide the Fertile Crescent (Iraq, Syria, Lebanon, Jordan, Palestine) between themselves and impose on us a colonial arrangement in the disguise of the mandate system established by the League of Nations. In 1948, under a "reactionary" Arab system, we lost a large part of Palestine to Zionism. In 1967, under the leadership of "revolutionary" Egypt, we lost the rest of Palestine to Israel, along with the Egyptian Sinai and Syrian Golan Heights. Arab and Syrian nationalism of all flavors, from the time of independence in the 1940s, was defeated as well. Sovereignty inevitably went the same way. There were victories, all the more remarkable for their rarity, like the 1956 Suez War that, with American help, saw a humiliating British, French, Israeli retreat. But defeat that is suffered so many times, in so many different ways, in such a short span of time, becomes a powerful explanation for our mess. It's also unsatisfactory, even escapist. There was war, and then there was defeat. We fought but we lost. We tried but we failed. We were sabotaged, backstabbed, outsmarted, outgunned, outnumbered.

But is there not more to our inheritance? Is there not complicity? We knew, didn't we, that our political parties and social movements didn't fight the good fight for us and lose honorably; that in their tender years, they turned, buckled, defected, succumbed. We instinctively knew to go beyond the usual nonsense about the miserable failure of nationalism and liberalism and socialism and secularism, and recognized that there was not much commitment to them to begin with. These "isms" were never allowed to germinate in the first place in order to be declared dead later.

This is, in fact, our accursed inheritance. We the elites—intellectuals, leftists, liberals, free-floating bourgeoisie, and aspirants to such glory—were complicit in our defeats. It's one thing when the powers that be have their way with us in spite of our best efforts; it's a calamity of a different magnitude altogether when we rip ourselves wide open to the carnage. This is the damnable legacy that led my generation to the desert and its silence.

Four giant ideologies and their troop of parties inspired Arabs before independence and well after it: Arab nationalism that called for one Arab nation; Syrian nationalism that envisioned the Fertile Crescent as indivisible; socialism and communism. They swept to power in some countries, their parties intertwining, splitting, mutating, and colliding. And then they failed in all.

But it wasn't the failure itself that chafed. Rather than overthrow the legacies of colonialism—the imposed borders, the manufactured entities, the planted contradictions, the distorted economies—they went on to entrench them. Swiftly bending the knee, they cheered on the military dictatorships. They became violent violators of the progressive notions they championed.

None of them, these ideologies and their regimes, could win Palestine back, but they abused its good name, as they squabbled and slung mud at one another. They not only fought frequently as enemy states and parties, but as brothers-in-arms too, in the same camp, happy to be pawns and spoilers, wasting precious resources and time. And when they did so, bloodshed was almost always the way disagreements were settled and power won. "The horrifying thing, before anything else, is the easy readiness of comrades to kill each other,"[1] laments Fawwaz Traboulsi about the violence within the ruling Socialist Party in Southern Yemen, the worst of it the 1986 bloodletting. He could have been writing about every other Arab party.

It's almost indecent of me to rely on such a compressed abstract of a very rich history just to make a point—a history that has its noble struggles, its heroes and martyrs, its poets and novelists, its revolutionaries and philosophers, visionaries and pioneers. I have my own White Hats in this procession of titans. But that's the thing, you see. In the end, all I can say is: there they were and here I am!

A line in Pankaj Mishra's *Age of Anger* lingers in my head: "Disorder remained the fate of many [colonized] nations that had been insufficiently or too fervidly imagined."[2] Perhaps our predicament as "insufficiently imagined" colonized nations was too burdensome and our ideologues overcompensated with romanticism and mythology, thinking them enough to make the imagined come true and sustain it long after. Perhaps in the frenzy of conception and ecstasy of birth, they judged the looming hurdles to be small and believed their strength to be Herculean. And when, very soon, challenges erupted and causes converged, we discovered the frailty of the wise and the fortitude of the wicked.

"Have you studied Antoun Saadeh?" he asked softly as was always his habit.

"No."

"Have you read his books?"

"No."

"Do you know his history?"

"Not really."

"Do you know the history of the party?"

"I know yours in it, kind of."

"Fine! Once you have done all these things, then you can criticize him, but always with respect."

I remember well that afternoon in my junior year at Georgetown University. Abu Fadi was walking down the corridor as I was cracking a silly joke about Saadeh, the founder of the SSNP, my father's old party, while lounging on the living room couch in our Amman home. It shouldn't have been a memorable encounter, really. It was just a lazy afternoon, a teenager's stupid joke, her papa's gentle rebuke. But somehow through the years it became, for me, a kind of marker; a very brief chat between a father and daughter that evoked the road traveled and all that was lost or shed to lighten up the load as time drew nearer to my own adulthood—to that afternoon. The zeal, the optimism, the threat of the noose, the lessons learned, and through it all, the ideals that go and the principles that remain.

As Abu Fadi asked me these questions, it occurred to me that he had never encouraged me to learn about Saadeh and the SSNP, the "hizb" as we called it for short. That's what old warriors do, isn't it? Instill in their progeny the same ardor for their beliefs? I was a student of history and politics; ours was a political house; our bookshelves were crowded with practically every work published about the Middle East. When I was tiny and invisible, all I did was listen to him in rapture. When I was grown up, politics, for me, was like playing ping-pong, another sport of papa's we picked up as soon as our heads inched above the table. But he never came to me with a book or a paper or an article about Saadeh or the ideology, and I don't know why I didn't ask him about it that day.

Perhaps I thought there was no point. We were in another chapter, and the party was all but dead to him, politics all but dead to us. At least in that form: agitated, subversive, organized, vastly ambitious, and dangerous. I did grill him recently in one of our many daily conversations about why he never suggested I educate myself about the "hizb." "But it's how I brought you up. I brought you up on the principles I cherished in it," he answered. "For me, that's all that mattered."

I think often of my father's letter to Fadi in 1967. When he wrote it, twenty years had passed since he joined the party; eighteen since Saadeh's summary execution by the Lebanese authorities in 1949; and five since his own death sentence. Fifteen years between the letter and my sarcasm in 1982. Thirty-five years, all in all. It's an awfully short time in which to lose so much. A little more than three decades between a recently independent Levant determined to overcome its colonial heritage, and a Levant all but crushed by it.

In the 1940s and '50s, the SSNP could beguile: the Fertile Crescent (or Greater Syria in the party's parlance) as one, fiercely secular and reaching for the sun. It attracted dazzling men, took seriously its female members, proposed to erase colonialism's disharmonies, separate religion and state, educate minds, and then, on the shoulders of an awakened Syrian nation, hug the sky. By 1980, the party was a strange mix of earnest believers, old souls, apparatchiks, and hired guns.

But if one just glossed over its history, the specter of this sorry end was already haunting the SSNP at its zenith. In the 1950s, the head of the party, George Abd al-Massih, a ghoulish man, actually took up a room in the house of Saadeh's widow, Juliette, and their three daughters. The family of al-Zaim (the leader) was the first family of the "hizb," he reasoned, and who better to watch over them than the party's head? He went on to excavate and hide the bones of Saadeh, because, as he told the family who asked for their return, "These are the bones of the Syrian Umma (nation)."[3]

Uncle George, as he liked to be called, was excommunicated from the SSNP in 1956. His authorization of the assassination of Adnan al-Malki, the deputy chief of staff of the Syrian army in 1955, was apparently a step too far. But soon after, in 1961, was the great watershed: an attempted coup d'état by the SSNP in Lebanon so clumsy it sputtered to a farcical finale almost as soon as it had started. My father and others in the High Council had opposed the coup. He was not a believer in military coups and was very suspicious of the timing of this one. Informants had alerted the Deuxième Bureau, Lebanon's military intelligence, about the plot as it was being hatched.

The party's leaders were promptly sentenced to death, among them my father, who was in Paris on business, training on the Caravelle plane. He had only recently started his aviation career, helping to found LIA, a private airline. With the support of secret sympathizers of the "hizb," of friends who were members and others who were not, he fled from Paris to the Ivory Coast, to Iran, to Kuwait, and finally came to rest in Jordan.

My father's story alone is interesting enough. All the elements of a *roman-fleuve* are there: a man from a humble family with a revolutionary fervor for politics and an aviator's enthrallment with the boundless azure above. At the age of sixteen, on seething landscapes, the boy becomes a member of a political party with aspirations as magnificent as his own; at twenty-one, he returns to Lebanon from New York, an aeronautical engineer. He enters 1961 with the most splendid of dreams, and by the end of it, he's on the run, leaving a pregnant wife and four children behind. He reaches safe shores, finally, and his wife follows on later by land with the children. He's waiting at the Jordanian border as she arrives. Actually, they missed each other, and met later at the Hilal Pharmacy in Amman, which is perhaps a better cinematic climax. There was now the faintest glimmer of a smile on Fortune's face, and by the end of the decade she was grinning the widest of grins. The days of the "hizb," with its grand projects and phantasms, were now no more than material for memoirs. Still, the man, not even forty, had his two loves in his life again. Politics and aviation cohabited rather well in his new world, but it is a betrayal in every way of the one that he had envisioned.

And here I am at my desk, typing away about him and them and us.

It's an Arab saga writ small, especially of that early era. In its ordeals, at least, our family was not unique. It was a time of glorious creation and ceaseless challenge in the region. An Arab order as pliant as clay in a sculptor's hands. To be a Syrian nationalist or a Ba'athist or an Arab nationalist or a communist or a socialist was much more than a political choice; it was a yearning to define the very essence of our being. In this bid, the SSNP would prove a terrible disappointment. But its arc, for Arab parties en masse, was like a reflection in a pond. For those conceived while in power, such as the one led by Gamal Abdel Nasser (a *mélange* of Arab nationalist fervor and pseudo-socialist recipes), the harsh verdict could be seen cruelly etched on Gamal's face in the aftermath of '67. For those parties that found a path to power through military coups, like the Ba'ath, the nosedive would be infinitely more tragicomic, not to say burlesque. The SSNP forever pined for power, never reaching it. But it can still claim the ideology and Saadeh. The party's reputation may be in tatters nearly everywhere, but both Saadeh, a true martyr to his cause, and some of his teachings hold up well enough on home turf. The Ba'ath Party has Michel Aflaq by contrast. And his tale, in death, is one for the ages.

When Aflaq, who cofounded the Ba'ath in 1943, died in 1989 in Iraq, Saddam Hussein, who had been the protégé of "the revered founding father" as a cub, gave Aflaq a magnificent Islamic burial, blue-domed mausoleum and all. I am not altogether sure that the notoriously obtuse Ba'athists understood the irony of an Islamic send off to a Christian man, and an alleged secularist at that. But to the rest of us—aka the multitudes that had endured a lifetime of Ba'athist hypocrisies and debasements—this farcical windfall was only the latest in an endless list of hilarious validations of chicanery. It's quite a feat, after all, to tumble from the cloud hugging peaks of Unity, Liberty, and Socialism, all the way down to the Iraq of Saddam.

Alas, for Aflaq, the story doesn't quite end with the Iraqi president's *Basmalah* prayer (*In the name of God, the Most Gracious, the Most Merciful*) over his grave. The gods must have been very amused by the spectacle and decided to do one better. This is how one contractor described Aflaq's mausoleum in 2006, three years after the American invasion of Iraq:

When you look inside, and before you get to the headstone, you pass a foosball table. Weights and a bench press are adjacent to the tomb. The US military has converted the interior to a rec room. A dusty chandelier is attached to the ceiling, which is decorated with a sort of faux-mosaic. The walls have been covered with wood, for reasons that are not immediately evident. Perhaps to allow for bookshelves? Two stairs lead down from either side of the grave to cramped, makeshift barracks constructed with plywood. There are dozens of soldiers who live beneath Aflaq's grave.[4]

By 2010 the mausoleum had morphed into a supermarket that sold "pirated DVDs, jogging suits and miniature carpets emblazoned with the words 'Operation Iraqi Freedom' to US soldiers and security guards from Peru and Uganda."[5] It's as if providence had its own bone to pick with Aflaq and just wouldn't let up with the insults.

It reads like pure *schadenfreude*. But truly it isn't. How dearly I wish our path was different and Uncle George and Comrade Michel were the exceptions rather than the rule. And how relieved and reassured I would have been had their example been unique to Greater Syria. As I wrap this section up, Yemen is ever present in my thoughts. There was a time when it barely registered with us. It was an enigma, so far away and tangential to our dilemmas. We knew it to be ancient, mesmerizing, the mother of us all, a place to visit and behold and savor. I was awestruck when Ali al-Jabri showed me his paintings of Sanaa's historic old city. It must have been in 2001, the year before he passed away. Visual poetry about a beautiful country I knew so little about. And to my shame it wasn't until 2011 that it began calling to me.

What I take from Yemen's story is what I take from my own as a Levantine. It didn't have to be this way—and it could well not have been. It's not only Southern Yemen's unique Marxist experiment between 1969 and 1986 that intrigues. It's the elements of bold change that were strewn like seeds on earth never to take root, languishing now as footnotes to an appalling trajectory. I pause at, say, Southern Yemen's Family Law of 1973 that declared genders equal, prohibited polygamy, and enshrined equality between men and women in divorce and custody. I pause again, in wonder, at the burqa (face covering) burning parties in the countrywide national festivals of 1976. And yet again, I pause at the chants in the Glorious Seven Days Marches of 1972: "Lowering salaries is a duty, the burning of chadors is a duty."* I pause at these examples of how our own future might have been written differently.

It's an Arab chronicle of constant conspiracies and unforgivable mistakes. Unforgivable not only because they were detrimental to our progress, but also because they were avoidable.

In *The Stillborn*, Arwa mentions how the '70s generation, in failure, would come to experience the contempt they heaped on the generation before them. I had scribbled in my copy by that paragraph: "Modern Arab history can be summarized as one generation heaping contempt on the one before it." It's a crude oversimplification, one meant for marginalia. And yet, as a succinct explanation for our reticence, contempt does seem rather compelling.

Politics, for us, was at once horror show and farce, the medium through which we watched the sheer weirdness of our overlords and their ideological retainers play out. It's not to say that there weren't good people in politics, but they simply were drowned out, didn't count, or didn't last. It was trench warfare and sniping all the time—intraparty, interparty, old guard, vanguard, military uniforms, neckties. By the '80s, you couldn't keep track, there were so many offshoots and renegades and fronts and acronyms, each servicing one or more sponsor. The more vital the cause, the dearer to our hearts, the more numerous the splinter groups. Palestine, the priciest merchandise by far, would here again take the brunt. We were swamped in a

---

*The marches were from the countryside to Aden calling for various socialist measures, among them the nationalization of housing and the lowering of privileged public sector salaries.

sea of parties: Fatah, PFLP, PFLP-General Command, DFLP, FRC, PLF, ALF, Fatah Uprising, As-Sai'qa, Islamic Jihad, Hamas. . . . We knew in our guts that Palestine, left in the hands of our rulers, would be lost, much as we knew by then that none of the parties—be they Nasserite Pan Arabism, the Ba'ath, the SSNP, the Communist Party, or any of their derivatives—had the wherewithal or inclination to realize the mammoth task of providing a modicum of dignity in our daily lives.

So we naturally absconded to three islands of the mind: the heretics like me, beyond any peddler's reach, who set up camp in no-man's-land; the mindless or cynical loyalists, for whom politics was nothing more than "hail-to-the-king"; and the true believers, the loneliest and most vulnerable of the three. This being the Arab world, quite a few of us in the second and third categories hopped often among these three isles, depending on the issue at play, the family situation, instructions from HQ, and other such cues. We warred, switched sides, or kissed and hugged because—well, such were the wishes of Caesar. In this, ironically, we were more or less in step with the restless ideological sages who were themselves actually doing nothing more than playing Simon Says.*

This cannot be a full accounting of our listlessness as a generation and our seemingly defeatist embrace of incrementalism. But, as I chisel away for answers, I find that even this partial account holds real promise.

I wouldn't want this chapter to read like a reckoning, though. I see little sense in finger pointing, not within these pages, at least. Clarity, for its own sake, is a beautiful thing. And it is clear to me that we fell into our pragmatism not only out of fear but also out of contempt for and absence of belief. Arab despotism might have been well served by the efficacies of these two motives, but they are not its handiwork alone.

---

*Children's copycat game.

CHAPTER 6

This Cannot Last

All the attention garnered by the Arab uprisings in recent years has left an important blind spot: the citizens who cling to some aspects of a regime even as they resent the system as a whole.

—Mortada al-Amin

The realization that I am an emotional cripple stood over me like a tut-tutting professor. I have a visceral unwillingness to grieve or patiently nurse loss. I deal with emotional pain through silent abandonment. I walk away, shaking emotional scraps off me like so many raindrops off my coat.

My much-prized compartmentalization techniques are all bogus, according to my therapist. I had, over quite a few sessions, been helpfully sharing them with her. I isolate the issue, address it, achieve closure, and move on. I am so good at it, I told her, that A2-G2 was a former boyfriend's *Star Wars* dig at me.* But just like that, what I was sure was a cherished, simple, plain-as-day fact about me was unmasked by her as another thatch of frailties and evasions. I was stumped.

I remain so, I suspect. An emotional cripple, that is. Realization in therapy is one thing, doing something about it in real life is a whole other ordeal. You'll understand, then, why I don't want to dwell on the Arab Spring and why this chapter is much shorter than it ought to be.

When Tarek el-Tayeb Mohamed Bouazizi set fire to himself, and Tunisia's Ben Ali's rule soon after burned with him, I rummaged around for that speck of hopefulness that I had mothballed deep

---

*R2-D2 (Artoo-Detoo), fictional robot character appearing in the *Star Wars* movies (USA franchise created by George Lucas).

in my psyche. I found it, wiped it clean of grime and dust, and carried it with me everywhere I went. By 2014, I had to wrap it up tight again and tuck it away along with the rest of my aspirations. Until further notice.

When Ben Ali fell, we demurred. Isn't Tunisia far away? Out of range? Much of what we have in abundance, it doesn't; much of what it has in abundance, we don't. A relatively small army averse to politics; a feisty labor movement; an assertive secularism, an accommodating Islamism. But, really, what did any of us know? Besides, Husni Mubarak, barely a few days after Ben Ali went down, reminded us that we had all been properly immunized. There was no risk of an Arab contagion. Tunisia was alone and lonely. A one-off.

When Mubarak fell soon after, I cannot give the exact count to a man and woman—nobody can—but I'll be goddamned if not millions of us collectively muttered to ourselves, "We can actually get rid of these people?" We could almost taste and smell the rot; it had sat soiled and fetid on us for so long. But it wasn't the stillness of the swamp. For years, we had seen and felt the slow burn of fury, ceaseless and riveting. Labor strikes, bread riots, episodic revolts, and demonstrations were erupting like rashes and outbreaks on the surface of the body politic like boils on human skin. But heads rolling? With such speed? So, by the time Bashar Assad experienced the Syrian people's own version of "leave," it was open season. The skeptics were suddenly quiet. You never saw so many caveats dangle from once-cocky opinions.

For three years, much seemed possible, even achievable. Political space was opening up in ways previously unimaginable. For all the smothering of decades past, and for all the scheming of the security apparatus and Islamists as the revolts gathered momentum, a different kind of politics was asserting itself. Progressive, young, post-Islamist, it appeared surprisingly audacious and nimble. It was glaringly unorganized, inexperienced, factional, and didn't quite know how to strive after what it wanted, but it certainly could mobilize, agitate, inspire, and it deployed social media like an arsenal. Independent labor unions and political parties were forming; agitation on factory floors, in squares, neighborhoods, and alleyways was growing bolder and louder; journalism was regaining its vitality.

It's understandable, then, that even the most cynical in our midst—and I gladly own up as one—thought something might just be giving way, that Arab despotism was weaker than it seemed and that outside powers might retreat long enough to let the uprisings breathe. It was the speed of the tyrants' falls that deceived. We thought if it were that easy to make them wobble or bring them down, surely their regimes would collapse before long.

We were wrong.

By 2014, we had become a patchwork of quandaries. The Fertile Crescent and North Africa were crazed and unfathomable; the Gulf was dazed and panicky. Only Tunisia remained tentatively reassuring. The region in no time at all morphed from the world's last bastion of stasis into its catacomb. Now, in 2022, desperately searching for solace, we find it only in the past, raw and hard most of it—for most of us. We pray that the worst is behind us, but we worry that the stars are saying otherwise.

Might there be an education in these very early years of havoc? Interpretations with a decent shelf life? Insights about this new generation of Arab rebels, about what we, the people, and our rulers have come to mean to one another?

Revelation No. 1: Be Careful What You Wish For

For me, there are four suspicions that became revelations after 2011. I'll start with "be careful what you wish for," because we must acknowledge the great debt we owe our regimes for being true to their word and nature.

All the usual culprits have had starring roles in our counter-revolutionary drama: foreign interference, the ambivalence of our revolutionaries, the absence of our organized politics, the complicity of our Islamist movements, the resilience of our police states. At each stage, they have performed for us terrifying acts of deception and betrayal, all very familiar in their sweeping themes and unbearably painful in their detail. But for Syrians, Libyans, and Yemenis, these performances have been cataclysmic. They pushed for change and their life turned into a living hell. Not just run-of the-mill misery but a Gehenna, where every memory of country, neighborhood, street, home, land, perhaps lover, husband, wife, child, parent, and sibling has turned into one soaked in blood and draped in black.

Syria, Libya, and Yemen: three prototypes of revolt, their preface euphoria, their epilogue dystopia. What started out as an arguably spontaneous, even timid uprising, unleashed demons that, once riled and bidden, have hideously iterated for each people a different version of "Mad Max." It beggars belief that a desire for better odds in life would summon wrath of such vigor, but as perplexing as it may be, the meaning of this cautionary tale is jarringly simple: it's either the regime or fire and brimstone.

What remains today, then? The people. They remain, but not necessarily where they would want to be. The names of countries and cities: these too remain. More or less, the borders as well—for the time being. The rest is a Homeric unfolding that has yet to settle into epic prose. For those Syrians, Yemenis, and Libyans who stayed, who are not condemned to be forever wandering (expats, refugees, migrants, asylum seekers, the dead), the absurd and macabre is the new normal, lived round the clock. A Syrian firefighter mentioned in a 2019 report offered this description of his situation:

The government wants soldiers, not employees. They don't really care how ordinary citizens are living. Our salaries don't exceed 20,000 pounds [approximately 40 dollars], so really we're working for God more than anything else. I'm the leader of a fire brigade and I still have to work as a taxi driver and depend on support from my family. Everyone in the brigade has another job.

The state bought our fire suits through a corrupt contractor, and you can tell the suits are basically plastic. In a serious fire I think

*they would melt on our bodies. We only have one driver for
our fire truck, so if he's not around when we need him, there's
nothing we can do.*[1]

Whole communities, once shepherded by a paternalistic
state, abandoned; and that same state now scavenges for scraps,
along with common folk. Realities part freakish, part wretch-
ed. We don't know which will dissipate or evolve with time and
which will resist and last. Certitudes here are sure to be mocked
until the *day after* finally arrives.

I fear many of us soon will begin to avert our eyes when we
land upon a painful photo or headline, the way we have learned
to do over Palestine and Iraq; such is the cornucopia of tragedy,
such is the prevalence of the paradoxical and bizarre.

Revelation No. 2: Know Your Regime

"Know your regime" has a special ring to it. You'd think this
is elementary, but it's actually an intricate affair, to know exactly what kind of tyranny is tyrannizing you. It may not make
much of a difference if you are simply trying to cope under it
day-to-day, but if your aim is to wrestle it to the ground, then
you had better go to the fight prepared. Because on the political
battlefield, *dictatorship* is a useless précis of oppression. It tells
you little, and offers you neither clues nor guideposts when the
hour is upon you.

What we have in much of the Arab world is a police state,
where a labyrinthine, shadowy, corrupt, nepotistic, predatory
security apparatus is the pivot and spine of the regime. This is
not your standard issue authoritarianism—the early, basic, expired model that hinges on the big guy. This is an adversary that
is a much more advanced, elaborate, diffuse, omnipresent, ten-
tacled creature. Soon after independence, it had its debut as a
junior partner, acting as the muscle, eyes, and ears of the leader
and his retinue. But as the rulers' appetite for control grew, as

their insecurities and rivalries multiplied, so did junior, mutating into two or three or even four likenesses of itself, acquiring more resources, larger influence, and greater stakes in the state, slowly developing a *raison d'être* all of its own. It wraps itself around *majesty* and its attendant cronies to shore them up or sink them, to hug them or strangle them. Its interests are both tied and not tied to the ruling clique. It's both in business and in politics, both for and against, at the top and at the bottom, above ground and below.

This police state is not one and the same everywhere. In different countries it takes on different features. But unavoidably, the military and security wings are at the nexus of this brand of tyranny, and once it takes root and ramifies, it becomes notoriously difficult to remove. In the event of a popular revolt, you have to catch its keepers in some sort of family dispute, or provoke one among them; they have to be desperate for cash; powerful foreign friends have to turn sour on them or at least become indifferent to their lot; and a key member in the apparatus would have to defect. Tricky anywhere. In the Middle East, good luck with that.[2]

Because that's who we are, where we are, what we have: a beleaguered people, a strategic location, a wealth of resources, Israel for a neighbor. It induces chronic anxiety and paranoia, a state of siege in our politics. It makes foreigners hungry for our riches and very forgiving of, even thankful for, our despots' worst instincts. Money pours into our security organs even as the rest of our institutions starve for lack of attention. And when competing foreign suitors decide that they have an interest in an internal conflict, which is almost always the case, the outcome is even more terrible. That's the way the Arab world turns, and just in case the implications eluded us before 2011, they have shown through with remarkable energy ever since.

There is any number of examples available to us. In Egypt, we watched Mubarak (who most thought was one notch below the Almighty himself) topple, only for the entire network under him to hold. He was promptly sacrificed. The Muslim Brotherhood, the only organized opposition, was encouraged to rend, distract, and thwart an undisciplined revolt, while the military, then resurgent within the police state, again won the edge for itself. It was messy, murky, high risk, sinister, but it happened. I wonder, though, would it have been quite the achievement without the billions that were injected into Egypt by the UAE, Saudi Arabia, and Kuwait when Abdel Fattah el-Sisi became president in 2013? Without the ensuing support of the IMF's $12 billion package in 2016? Had Sisi had no access to financial relief, or if it had come, say, with instructions for him and the army to stick to a military career, how might his presidential fortunes have turned? How might those of the uprising? Or Egypt's?

I simplify shamelessly to particularize an Arab muddle, but there is nothing even deceptively formulaic about it. Its rightful name is "predicament." Complexities, contradictions, ambiguities, uncertainties, and shifting realities suffuse it, much like hallucinations may crowd a schizophrenic's mind. In real time, in the confusion of the day and the sweat of the night, we the people are left to sift through the rumors, pick through the conspiracies, consult our Turkish coffee cups, share Facebook posts, videos, and tweets, talk incessantly, and seek information from connected friends in the hope that they might offer us a hint of what is being cooked up—or not. And, of course, what goes for us goes double for those active in the revolts.

As I write this, I am experiencing it in Beirut on November 23, 2019, with the country in freefall, and we all feel like Peeping Toms. It's been a month since a seeming blanket refutation of a ruling class that has restyled basic rights into sectarian favors, plundered the country, and made of us peddlers and beggars, chasers and bribers, Houdinis and fabulists, accomplices and targets. Four weeks into the protests, we know much and we know practically nothing. We scour for clues and inside scoops, not unlike addicts looking for their next fix.

So, what's a rebellion, if that is what it really is, to do in the absence of light?

What's a bastard rebellion to do? No vanguards nor rearguards; no ideology nor party; no structure, organization, or identity—yet. Just mass furor staring at walls and locked doors, a cry from the heart that this cannot last.

What's it to do with emblems of "revolutionary" failure—Egypt, Syria, Libya, and Yemen in the rear view—and portents of irrepressible rage in Algeria, Sudan, and Iraq in the foreground? What's it to do in a Lebanon whose sectarian and economic elite has managed to pull together a political order of extraordinary resilience? A Lebanon perennially beholden to foreign patrons, whose interests may be obvious but whose moves are understood only in hindsight; caught between Iran, Syria, Israel, Saudi Arabia, and Turkey nearby, and the US, Russia, and France never too far off, all with agendas by turns intersecting and clashing, singular or multiple, depending on the week and the month. What's this rebellion to do? As Iran and the US take to the floor for this latest dance, the first sanctioned, financially squeezed, and unexpectedly vulnerable in Lebanon and Iraq; the second a mighty, capricious country heedful only of Israel's needs and wants. The one very close and with the patience of Job, the other far away and with a notoriously short attention span.

What's this rebellion to do?

Revelation No. 3: The Emperor Has No Clothes, and Neither Do We

I cannot give the exact count to a man or woman—nobody can—but I'll be goddamned if millions of us, by 2015, had not muttered to ourselves, "We will never get rid of these people." I don't know how many of us mutterers were above the age of forty, but I am willing to hazard we were the majority. If in 2011, we followed the youth to the streets, by 2015 we led the queues out. We tend to take it on the chin; they are happy to take it in the chest. Understandable. Our day was back when and—well, as I wrote—we passed. And, why deny the obvious? It's their fight now, against conditions much worse than ours were then: malfunctioning states, no job or business to be had, depressed wages when they are, no security in which to bring up a family, no rights, and, ominously, no West or Gulf to welcome them in droves anymore. So, they begin to stir toward the end of the century, become even more restless by the beginnings of the new one, and finally rise in 2011. We follow, perhaps out of guilt and shame and the need to feel that we can make a difference this time around. We all fail in the first run, and just when the region's custodians think that we have all absorbed the lesson of "be careful what you wish for," at that very moment when they think they have crushed the revolt in Egypt, Syria, Yemen, and Libya, the rebels rise again, this time in Algeria and Sudan, in Lebanon and Iraq.

Which ushers the third revelation of 2011: "the emperor has no clothes, and neither do we." There are no pretenses anymore; no pretense of a real bond, a serious promise, or common cause. It's a nakedly honest relationship between ruler and ruled. They no longer pretend to care for our wellbeing, because who would believe them? And we no longer pretend to love them, because who would believe us? It's a bare, bare Arab political terrain. Every grand idea and party and movement that lit up the twentieth century survives only as a relic in the twenty-first century. Even Palestine, once the defining trauma of our time, is now but one of many that scar us. Sovereigns and Islamists of every color and bent are hobbled in pairs, the first creating the vacuum that the second is all too ready to fill. It's not to say that they no longer have their diehards, but there is nothing at all in this bleak proposition for the rest of us.

Revelation No. 4: Are These Rebels Revolutionaries or *Refo*lutionaries?

Over the past few weeks, I've been thinking of the plights that bind in this era of breakups. I notice, for example, that the old tradition of farewells in massive generational convoys is over. I look no farther than my family and friends. Cousins in the Ivory Coast, Zimbabwe, and Senegal, all courtesy of my maternal grandfather, who went to Africa in 1920 and his two sons who decided to stay on. Cousins in the US, Canada, London, and Sweden on my father's side. Nieces and nephews in New York, London, and Dubai; friends in London, Paris, and Dubai. None of them coming back.

The departed. That's us. Nations of migrants. By sheer numbers alone, we depict a story of flight. Three times the world average in eight Arab countries in 2012.[3] But no more. When we pack, we will be packing because we have a specific talent, a skill set, a foreign passport, or an abundance of money.

I notice other things as well. I notice the apparent restraint of the young rebels. Which brings me to the fourth revelation of 2011, this time in the form of a question: "Are these rebels "*refolutionaries*" (to borrow Asef Bayat's term) or revolutionaries?"[4] They want social justice, dignity, and bread, but reforms seem to do it for them. They don't want to raze the system root and branch; they just want to slap it awake, push it to sacrifice a face or two, get its act together, clean itself up, and get on with the business of good governance. They want fair electoral laws, an independent judiciary, a clampdown on corruption, freedom of expression and thought, jobs, decent wages, better education and health care, housing, clean air and water ... but they want our potentates to own up and do their part.

At first look, it's akin to aiming for the moon on a donkey cart.

Are these rebels, then, glorified NGOers as many of their critics label them—"deradicalized activists" and orphaned leftists speaking the language of "human rights, political accountability, and legal reform"?[5] A generation made practical and flexible, much like mine. But we were solicitous and feeble because the state was still robust, neoliberalism was young, and the exits were many; they are insistent and loud because the state is spent, neoliberalism is exposed, and the exits are down to none. Or do they also know in their heart of hearts that the time of revolutions of old, of Che Guevara and Ali Shariati, is gone? And so, they "no longer seek to overthrow regimes as in the 1970s and 1980s. Instead they intend to transform them from within. . . ."[6] Do these rebels believe that this is the best they can do under a merciless police state? Do they, in fact, *know their regimes* very well, their own limitations even more, and set their conditions just so, to be implemented in the spirit of win-win? But then, in a climate that humbles protestors into merely asking for concessions and encourages states to cede little, what starts out as low volume agitation soon grows into a piercing crescendo that surprises even the protestors themselves.

Was this not the path to the 2011 and 2019 revolts? All whistles and bells. Egypt, by 2011, a hotbed of malcontents.[7] A red arrow shooting upward across industries, classes, and cities. There were twenty-seven annual actions on average between 1988 and 1993, which jumped to 118 between 1998 and 2003, and hit 265 in 2004. Two to four million Egyptians had joined one strike or another between 1998 and 2011.[8] Algeria became a factory of riots—13,000 of them in 2017 alone.[9] Sudan had been in ferment since 2013. You study countries, you visit them, you dutifully mark the differences by function of history, of politics, of norms, geography, resources, of the million tiny peculiarities and idiosyncrasies that make a people distinct, but you register a shared feature across the Arab region: the collapsing order of things.

Does this at least partly explain the "peaceful transitions" that "re*fo*lutionaries" appear to want? In Egypt, they entreat the army to chaperone them. In Tunisia, they cohabit with a still powerful old guard. In Syria, before it all blew up, they call for generals "who don't have blood on their hands" and for new presidential elections. In Sudan, they agree to work with war criminal Mohammed Hamdan Dagalou. In Lebanon, they tell the sectarian hierarchy it has failed, then demand that it oversee its own dismantlement, as if to say, you broke it, you fix it. They call for change, mobilize for it, but they don't seize it because they don't know how, they don't have the strength, the experience, the organization, the support, the taste for blood. Because they are the children of war and its heartbreaks in Sudan, Algeria, Lebanon, and Iraq. Because they instinctively know violence is our regimes' darkest wish, what they want most and do best. Because they have a visceral suspicion of politics, a hatred of it, in fact, inculcated in them. An instinctive mistrust of anyone who aspires to it, who has the taste for it. When I propose this to a prominent Lebanese activist, he nods. But what to do? He has his work, an NGO to look after, employees to take care of, salaries to pay, projects to launch, proposals to write. "Who am I, anyway?" he says. Down there in the squares and streets, in a freewheeling space of seminars, chats, and gazebos, with an army of groups and a mass of individuals from everywhere, who am I to say we do it this way?

These stadia of revolt, these arenas are for songs and for slogans. Demands that come in social media posts and graffiti find solutions in town hall meetings and WhatsApp video clips, not in pamphlets and treatise. The moment is for venting and heckling, naming and shaming politicians, their business partners, and their families, in restaurants and shopping malls, at the gates of parliament, and as close as the demonstrators can get to their offices and houses. Strategy is a has-been. Tactics rule. "The people demand, they don't negotiate," I keep being reminded on my WhatsApp feed by nonrepresentatives of "the people."

In this space, even as the winter and cold descend, the tents are the gathering places of would-be citizens brought together by a shared goal or grievance. That's no small achievement in Lebanon, my activist friend says. I nod. I know this is just the first of many rounds, he says, but we have managed to plant seeds. And that's no mean feat. I catch myself thinking of those seeds of Southern Yemen in 1973, of Egypt in the 1950s, of Lebanon, Syria, and Iraq in the 1950s and 1960s—so too of Jordan. Who am I to second-guess this moment, I chide myself? I remember the euphoria I felt in 2011, in Martyrs' Square in 2019; the chants and songs, the heated conversations and laughter, the sense of anticipation—even when I knew better. However fleeting, it's a feeling of liberation like no other, as Arwa Salih wrote; of heroism, of luminosity and giddiness. Surely it deserves to belong in our memory; surely it deserves its place in this journey.

Over the short term, it will be bad, very bad. Over the medium term, I am kind of optimistic, he says. I think to myself, define "medium."

It's January 2020. I received yesterday a WhatsApp from my activist friend. The march on Saturday from Dawra, in East Beirut, to the Banking Association downtown—hours by car, 30 minutes on foot—was big. The protests, it would appear, are picking up again. In his message is a subtle allusion to our discussion a few weeks ago. "The situation is turning more political." He ends with, "I am optimistic."

That's all I want to say about the Arab uprisings.

CHAPTER 7

The Tourist

There are things that can only be understood retrospectively, when many years have passed and the story has ended. In the meantime, while the story continues, the only thing to do is tell it over and over again as it develops, bifurcates, knots around itself. And it must be told, because before anything can be understood, it has to be narrated many times, in many different words and from my different angles, by many different minds.

—Valeria Luiselli

How to tell a tale about endings? How to tell it to friends and strangers alike, for there are those who recognize much and those who know little, if anything? How to tell it with nuance for good company and sparse prose for breathing space? I read the first draft yesterday. Dense as pumpernickel. So, I begin again.

Barely a couple of weeks after my arrival in Beirut in 1991, I rode down from a dinner party in Beit Meri with Riad, a friend. He took us through the center of town for a fly-by-night tour. As we entered at a crawl, buildings stood crucified on both sides of the road; an honor guard to the horror show about to unfold. For a few minutes, we were alone, two people gaping at the hideousness of human strife. Only Riad's voice, guiding me through the images, and the wheels grinding on gravel pierced the night's hush. In matters of war and its special kind of death of places and human beings, I was naïve. I sat still, eyes flitting between vistas of rubble, imagining the dead bemoaning a life so needlessly and cruelly cut short. Then, in the near distance, an eye-level faint light shone. As we approached, we saw coffins in different sizes and types of wood in the lone workshop. In it was an old coffin maker carving his way through another abode for the hereafter.

In the very early hours of "peace," in the dead of night, in a cemetery of everything wondrously Lebanese, the only human activity was a retail business to permanently house cadavers. Had I had a camera on me. If only.

Lebanon lives and dies by its howling juxtapositions. They are what gives it such license and makes it such a fraud. Before the 1975–90 Civil War, people marveled at how a tiny mosaic of a country, of 10,452 square kilometers, was somehow the belle of the ball. They marveled even more at the scintillating contrasts that made us special: the lush geography of towns and cities peppering the seashore and mountains, so near to one another and yet so far, strangers and siblings at the same time; the way we embrace our every sensibility and its antithesis; the way our beguilingly malleable selves are bathed in nuance. All, the rich and delicate embroidery that thread every inch of our troubled identity in this tiny, tiny country.

It would prove our undoing that our strengths are our defects, our exceptionalism our vulnerability, our enviable location our tender spot. Before 1975, we were a sanctuary for the Arab world's literati and a den for its intrigues, a magnet for certain talents and a brain drain for many more, heedlessly wide open to the world and stubbornly exclusionary within our own. Cosmopolitan on weekdays, parochial on weekends, entrepreneurial and yet incapable of seeing beyond our own nose, urbane and uncouth, playful and thin-skinned, cultured and bigoted. Did I mention we are a tiny, tiny country?

This way... and that! Eternal rivals. Inseparable. Each equally real, good and bad. None of it was inevitable, just the pattern of history, part choice, part happenstance, part destiny, inside and out, just like everywhere else. And in our modern formation— petite, coastal and mountainous, stunning all around, politically feeble, economically cliquey, confessionally diverse, culturally colorful, habitually flirtatious, instinctively opportunist—it made us essential. Essential here, in the Arab world. And intolerable. Because Lebanon is where the hounded Arab poets and novelists, political dissidents and journalists came "in search of something: solidarity with the Palestinian resistance, a refuge from persecution, the promises of modernity, the discovery of self, the affirmation of individuality, the possibility of citizenship and the dream of freedom."[1] Not a day passed when you wouldn't spot them at cafés like the Horse Shoe and L'Express. Not a summer passed when you wouldn't spot the Arab bourgeoisie frolicking at the Cave du Roi, lounging at the St. Simon Beach, and vacationing in high up Sawfar and Aley. But here as well came friend and foe to do mischief with very little cost to themselves. Here is where celebrities and spies mingled at the bar of the St. Georges Hotel.

Lebanon is where the Arab pen was at its freest and where Arab despots went on bribing and killing sprees to quell dissent. Where Palestinian refugees seemed like the only unwelcome guests, languishing, along with other invisible Lebanese, in our poverty belts. But so powerful was "intoxicating Lebanon" as a brand that joie de vivre became the singular quality of a country where life was actually bad for the ubiquitous human detritus of inequity airbrushed out of the photo op.

> *Even if we were to concede, for argument's sake, that the first impression that comes to mind when we remember those days is wrapped in nostalgia, this does not belie the fact that Beirut then was a city that throbbed and no one could catch up with it or compete with the way it mesmerized. . . . It's as if . . . when the fairies wanted to disburse gifts to Arab cities, they agreed to make Beirut the base of the good life.*[2]

So wrote Samir Kassir of the jewel in the Arab crown that shimmered between 1948 and 1975.

But I wonder whether Beirut, against a different backdrop, would have been anything more than an intriguing little haunt? For all its beauty and charm and cleverness and libertine tastes, would it have sparkled so brilliantly had Damascus and Baghdad, Cairo and Alexandria, been allowed to stay truer to their characters and pedigrees? Had our regimes not been cruel and stern and insecure and spiteful; had Haifa and Jaffa and Jerusalem not disappeared behind the Israeli fence? Would we Lebanese, we Beirutis, have basked so confidently in our specialness and suffered so immeasurably at its hands?

Useless exercise, "what if." You can't throw the dice on one fact without having to bet the entire farrago of events. After every futile attempt, the only thing that remains is a feeling of sorrow and wistfulness. And still, we Lebanese, in this realm of regrets, confound. We confound in how well we clung to the magic in the full glare of the war's devastation; how we held on tightly to those hallmarks that had always sustained the pretense. And with hardly any effort. After the bloodshed, we just reveled in even more frighteningly jarring juxtapositions, confident that the world would be as forgiving of our foibles as we were ourselves.

When the conflict ostensibly ended in 1990, we just substituted old contrasts with new. Many of the landmarks were fast fading or gone—the St. Georges, the age-old souks, the Horse Shoe (the intellectuals' lair), Sawfar and Aley. Hamra Street. We also lost our beautiful sea, the stone architecture and red brick roofs that gave our villages and towns a memory and made of the view a magnificent Mustapha Farroukh painting, the orange blossom that hinted to my mother that she was approaching Sidon. . . . Now, on a tattered Lebanese canvas we had sectarian warlords and their fiefdoms, jungles of concrete, animal carcasses and feces soup in the sea, buried chemical waste, pulverized quarries, garbage, and landfills.

This is the way of most fratricides, it is true. They have their price tags, usually variations on the above. But in Lebanon, it quickly became clear that there would be no meaningful transition from ruin to repair; that the markers of our war would also be those of our peace. "Militia" economies would quickly take root as the new economy of "reconciliation and reconstruction." Lebanon would be divvied up into princely dominions. And the chieftains, with their carpetbaggers in tow, would all be in on the spoils. By law and norm, sectarianism would lodge in every nook and cranny of the state. The feud certainly had its perceived winners and losers, but they were a mere detail of the much larger and consequential outcome of the conflict. The sectarian setup held, with its parochial character, oligarchic economy, casual corruptions, monopolistic tendencies, and addiction to sugar daddies, local and foreign. And atop what amounted to our Second Republic, Syria would preside as custodian. Political and economic deformities nurtured in the mayhem would thus come into their own in the apparent calm, and all that ailed Lebanon before and during the war would be even more tightly woven into the very fabric of our lives.

If we didn't suspect this in the first year of respite, we did in the second, or third, or fourth at the most. The misdeeds were naked to the eye, brazen, every day. So we surmised that we'd better attach a flourish to each flagrant mess—a *yes, but*—to lighten or confuse the real meaning of things, and we continued to celebrate the clashing narratives as a quintessential Lebanese marvel. Because if our excesses and contradictions weren't wondrous, what could they possibly be, if not a harbinger of our impending end? Basically, we spun grand theater from a shit show.

The sheer physicality of this Lebanese fable stuns. It's all sensory, visual. A construction of images in batches of two, the second always lifting the spirit right when it's about to irretrievably sink. Every set piece has somewhere within it another that quarrels with it as if to restore, in the midst of wholesale chaos, our faith in the Lebanese flair for survival and fun.

We have the easy couplings. On the edge of West Beirut's urban clutter, a hodgepodge of nondescript and unsightly high rises sits hidden behind wall-to-wall gardenias the Centrale restaurant, a magnificent concrete and iron homage to Brutalist architecture. In Batroun toward the north, the Jammal Restaurant and its small "pristine" bay curl up, only miles from huge patches of brown organic sludge. In Tyre, in the presence of the Islamist, Shiite movement, Hezbollah (aka the Party of God), runs a stretch of cool beachfront bars.

And then we have the very tired couplings. Perhaps the most clichéd of these is the 10-minute car ride between "Hezbollah's Southern Suburbs"—Dahieyh—and Sky Bar by the sea. Martyrdom and hedonism cheek by jowl, each content to leave the other well alone. The Jihaddis of Tripoli and Akkar in the north and the "bimbos" of downtown Beirut, with an hour's car ride between. Two fixtures in every other Western article about East and West, love of death and love of life, atavism and modernity, the veil and the miniskirt. Tucked neatly under them, the harsh backwoods and the sultry burg, the provincial inlands and the worldly coast, the tribe and the unfettered self, repressiveness and liberty. Tensions you come across nearly everywhere somehow acquire a miraculous pairing in Lebanon. Word-weavers just can't hold back their swooning odes to a place that is like nowhere else. It's a riddle for a little while; at least it was for me. But soon enough, the simple matter of proximity offers the light. It's not the contrasts per se that elicit such poetry; it's that they rub so intimately against each other in such cramped settings and still seem to cohabit. In a human being, acute polarities suggest illness, someone torn, unsettled, unwell. In this tiny, tiny country, they are the very qualities that make it sing.

Lebanon's pining lovers can go on forever with these duets. For them, there is no act of lamentation that does not come with its own redemption. Here's Dominique Eddé as recently as 2019, when all was said and done:

> You are in the city center, you stroll down a sidewalk eighteen inches wide, assailed from all sides by the confusion of buildings and traffic, torn between the appeal of the sea and the stench of garbage, and suddenly your gaze is soothed by the play of light on a stone wall, by bougainvillea cascading from an ancient balcony, by the balcony itself.[3]

Unfathomably, a generic image encountered in any other beautiful city fast succumbing to man-made environmental butchery is dubbed by Eddé as uniquely revelatory in Beirut. But then, in *The Compatibility of Opposites*, she does open with "Lebanon is both the center of the world and a dead end,"[4] subconsciously, I suspect, betraying the distance between what many Lebanese think about our country (the center of the world) and what it is in reality: a dead end.

Those who never fell hopelessly in love with this Lebanon— and there are a few of us—are invariably mystified at such serenades. We shouldn't be. It is nothing more than the object of love being idolized in futile love affairs that long ago stopped making sense, if they ever did. This is not to say that Lebanon was never worth loving. Exactly the opposite. But perhaps the biggest folly of those who claim to have loved it dearest was always to love it in bits and pieces. Theirs. Could things have been different? Very. Had they been much less forgiving of their Lebanon and themselves, had they loved it less, much less. Had they, in fact, hated it, we might have been able to save it.

For me, that is the only Lebanese paradox that has ever mattered.

For me! Me, the outsider, the visitor, the tourist, the one who left, who doesn't know, who is not in love; all nicknames given to me by acquaintances and friends, the insiders, the survivors, those who stayed, who know, who are in love.

What did I know of Lebanon back then? Hardly anything, according to them. Lebanon may be small, but it's small like a tight ball of yarn, easy to behold as a whole, but inscrutable on the inside. And, you see, it's the unraveling that is the poetry, according to them. Anyway, what do I remember of the Lebanon of the 1960s and '70s, I ask myself? Hardly anything beyond a montage of recollections that shaped an early, terribly vague sense of me and being. I lived here in 1967 and 1970–71. I visited every summer before the war and every once in a while during the fighting. We had an apartment in Hadath, a town toward the southeast of Beirut in the district of Baabdah. It was mainly middle-class Christian, mostly Lebanese. My paternal grandparents and aunts lived 10 minutes away in the three-story building my grandfather built with some help from his children, his end-of-service indemnity, and some savings. It was at the end of the street to the left as you went in, a clay beige color, as if a mock-up. Every twilight, the cul-de-sac turned into an outdoor café for the adults. Laughter and chatter, beer and bizr (sunflower seeds). By 7 o'clock, *Tele Liban* prepared to take over the night, coiffed presenters in black and white, in sing-song classical Arabic, ushering in *Bonanza* and *Abu Milhem*.*

Abu Milhem was a folkloric Lebanese show; *Bonanza*, an American cowboy series.

My family's street was uphill. At the top to the left lived Bassam, a Palestinian refugee in a small makeshift house. He's one of those childhood friends whose perennial gift is to anchor a memory in a time and place and dress it from head to toe in tender sentiment. I cannot think of Hadath without thinking of Bassam. Maybe because he never made it out of my past after 1971. A few years ago, he tracked down Fadi in Amman. He had packed up for Canada in the early 1980s, he said, and became an *oud* player with a music troupe. Michel was another childhood friend—stick thin, weak heart, pants ironed stiff, long-sleeved buttoned up shirt, fine, gelled hair combed sideways. He didn't make it past ten. Every other week, someone died in Hadath, it seemed, and every so often someone too young. Freak accidents or some such. At the end of our own alley lay an ancient priests' cemetery. We raided it often for trinkets and thrills. I would stand on the wall as guard while my brother, Bassam, and others jumped in. Once they came back with a derelict door. We liked to believe it was a coffin lid. Down the street we raced on it for weeks, turned now into a cart on iron wheels. Drunkard Edmond owned the bodega by the entrance of our building. We used to steal gum and chocolates and whatnots from him, open a "pop-up" a few meters away and sell the merchandise to the neighborhood's children. It was easy to steal from Edmond, with the rolled-up pants, purple blotches, and brown plastic slippers. Eight of us would swarm his tiny shop, a few would distract him while the rest amassed the goods. When my parents came back from a trip to Japan in 1971, they brought us the laugh machine, an electric toy that gave off the sound of a cackling man. We would secretly play it to Edmond, and he would start screaming at us for letting loose chickens in the store.

The doctor of the area was Pierre Dakkash. He was also a member of parliament. I would often hear the grownups saying he's the only clean and decent parliamentarian in the house. I heard that same thing said about him when I came back in 1991. I asked my father today why Hadath? All these years I never asked. The family was already there, he said, close friends from the "hizb" as well.

In the two years we were in Beirut in 1967 and 1970, school was Green Field College in Ghbayreh, a leafy district crossed by wide well-groomed streets and dotted with handsome Mediterranean buildings. The school was a mélange of Lebanese and other Arabs, mostly from the Gulf. The Sabra and Shatila Palestinian refugee camps were very near, tucked well behind the mass of trees. On the weekends, we rarely ever went south. We had little reason to, since my mother's connections were faded, and were nonexistent for my father. My maternal grandparents did keep their house there, in Nabatiyeh, even though they had long ago migrated to the Ivory Coast, but it was Umm Mussbah, my grandmother, who would come to visit in Beirut, driving her old Opel like a mad woman. Ismail (Abu Ali), my paternal grandfather, had relocated to Beirut in his teens in the early 1920s and left little of him and his in the south, and Umm Ali, my paternal grandmother, was actually from Sarafand by the seafront, around 60 kilometers on the southern road from the capital.

In the summers, we swam at the Beach Club or Siesta in Khaldeh, also toward the south. In the winters, we cozied up in the living room after school toasting cheese sandwiches on the kerosene heater. Ja'afar, the husband of my aunt Suoad, had a bookstore in 'Azarieh, in the old souks. Whenever we went there, he would give me children's books that I would read and put back in their elegant wrappings. Twice a year, my mother would bring us to Cacharel and Zahar in Hamra to shop for new clothes. On Sundays, she would take us in the early evening to Tirol, a terraced restaurant in Raoché on Ras Beirut's Corniche. The breeze, the dusk, the twinkle of lights, the sea. My hamburger and ice cream.

Cross the street and before you stood Beirut's famous Pigeon's Rocks. Down from that sidewalk lovers would descend, away from the public eye, to fall in love; others tragically less content would jump to their death.

When we went back to Amman in 1971, we let go forever of Hadath. On visits, we stayed in hotels. My grandparents and aunts left in 1977. They didn't feel welcome anymore. In 2010, after nineteen years of "peace," the municipality adopted an unwritten regulation: no leases or property or land sales to Shiites. Too many already, said the mayor, threatening sectarian "coexistence."

I have not been to Hadath since 1974. I visit the south only to mourn and bury the dead.

To be the "tourist" in my birthplace; to be the outsider almost everywhere in it and for nearly everyone I meet. I know practically nothing. I, the one who left. According to them, the ones who stayed. And maybe they're right. How could books ever be enough? So, I watched and listened. Time, war, absence, they all dictate their own estrangements from home for the wanderer, but the withering effect of bloodletting on the human condition was shocking. In fact, almost everything about Lebanon was shocking. It shocked me, not them. Those who had stayed. Nothing shocked them. That, perhaps, was my first valuable insight. The second one was how pleased they were with their hard shells; that no wrong would throw them off, trip them up, provoke doubt. I quickly learned as well that when the country went quiet in 1990, the hard shells, who, it seemed to me, far outnumbered the "tourists," just wanted to get the country running again, so that they could all ride it into the sunset.

Enter Rafic Hariri, or Sheikh Rafic, as everyone took to calling him in deference. When he finally got his dearest wish and became prime minister in 1992, the story was that we would all now sleep soundly on silk (*harir* in Arabic, a play on his last name). The contractor tycoon promptly set out to put in place the architecture of the Second Republic. There was nothing imaginative in the design, nothing remotely thoughtful or restrained, either. The old system would simply be refurbished and the war's disfigurements, sectarian and economic, would be normalized and bedecked with Haririan and neoliberal embellishments. Financing it would be a cocktail of massive debt, bloated interest rates, remittances, and the sacred 1,500 Lebanese lira to the US dollar fixed peg. Protecting it would be a tight partnership between our confessional and business class. Selling it would be braggadocio, glitter, and fireworks. Encasing it would be the state, under a canopy of sectarian benefits and services. The mood was festive, the carve-up was for all to see. It was public, official, boastful even, as they all congratulated themselves on ingeniously skipping a painful process of catharsis and reckoning, going instead directly to reward and gluttony.

Soon, even good people—people who knew better—would find themselves going with the flow, intrigued by the possibilities and cavalier about the implications. One evening in those early days of "prosperity," I was having dinner with a friend. He was a very successful businessman in his fifties who had left for the Gulf well before the Lebanese went for each other's throats. A well-educated scion of a prominent Lebanese-Palestinian family, he was, to all those who knew him, decent and hard working. That evening, he told me that he had just met with Elie Hobeika, one of the Maronite Lebanese Forces' commanders during the mayhem, whose résumé includes the 1982 massacre of Palestinian refugees in Sabra and Shatila. At the time of our dinner, Hobeika, who was assassinated in 2002, was minister of water resources and electricity. My friend proceeded to share with me how impressed he was with the minister, describing him as highly intelligent and very competent. Stunned, I said to my friend, "Since when is our problem with Hobeika that he is stupid or incompetent? We have a problem with him because he is a murderer, a war criminal." By the awkward look on my friend's face, it was clear that this fine point had somehow slipped through his filters. How, I do not know.

Like this, practically the entire upper crust of Lebanese society was swept up in the revelry, overtaken by the audacity and pizzazz of Hariri and tickled to death by the apparently miraculous resurrection of the country. It was a form of hysteria, a kind of desperate hankering for the good times to roll, with no patience for the hard work of healing the wounds of a gutted state and a traumatized society.

All kinds of excesses began to adorn public life, like show-cases of cheap wares in a bazaar. Everywhere we looked, there were garish displays of extravagance and crookedness. For the naysayers, Solidere (Société Libanaise pour le Développement et la Reconstruction du Centre-ville de Beyrouth), the Shiekh's brainchild, became the cause célèbre. The wholly private compa-ny was conceived by the late prime minister to own and control the most strategic real estate in the capital. He wanted to leave his mark on this sweet earth, he wanted to be known as the man who rebuilt Beirut and restored Lebanon's glory, he said, and there was no possession more vital to his ambition and more everlasting than the beating heart of it. So, he took it in the glare of day, in Parliament. He did not have to declare it for all of us to be sure that palms were greased and big favors were dispensed to secure the votes. His argument was that the property owners in the central district were too many and quarrelsome, dead or absent. He insisted the state was broke and paralyzed by petty interests and red tape, and he (and Lebanon) simply could not wait for it to get back in shape. At which point, inquisitive minds were asking why he would ever want to be prime minister of such a sorry place?

Without further ado, Solidere was awarded the center of town. It was authorized by the state to confiscate the center's private property, set the price for it, pay for it in shares, and ad-judicate proprietors' petitions. The state had thus, astoundingly, relegated itself to a bystander in one of the most critical transac-tions in Lebanon's modern history. Soon Hariri's vision of the new downtown, an assemblage of very expensive real estate, where only the rich could work, play, eat, and live, made obvi-ous his intentions to break with the spirit and urban texture of the old one, where people from everywhere would mingle and mesh. At the time, there was pushback from property owners, prominent architects and civil engineers, urbanists and arche-ologists, politicians and activists, journalists and intellectuals. Detailed critiques were presented, calls were made for inclusive multidisciplinary symposia, and alternatives were proposed to save the heritage of the area. But for the prime minister and his entourage, it was really a very simple either/or—it's either our way or bust; you're either for rebuilding Beirut or for killing it.

He won. And venting done, we soon grew used to Solidere; so used to it, in fact, that we stopped calling the city center by its actual name, *wasat al-balad*. I work in Solidere, I live in Solidere, I am heading for Solidere, right next to Solidere, we got used to saying. We ate in restaurants there, shopped, rented offices on Foche or Waygand or El Amir Bechir, bought apartments in Saifi Village. I did. My friends did. For years, we would complain to each other about sleepless nights, not out of guilt, but because it felt as though the place was hexed. Disturbed spirits that wouldn't let us be.

The neighborhood itself was just odd. It still is. A block of contemporary buildings constructed to feign age and painted in a rainbow of colors, it sits prettily on the higher edge of Martyrs' Square. It's supposed to mimic the feel of an old *quartier* but can't quite shake off the look of Legoland. Practically anything that starts up there soon enough shuts down.

Hexed! Jinxed! Whatever. But not all businesses have been condemned so. Meat the Fish, a high-end gourmet shop and eatery, the Backburner Café, The Core, an exercise boutique, and Paname Restaurant all breathe some life into Saifi's very narrow cobblestone streets. But, again, something is odd. Meat the Fish has dollhouse-size white wood tables and chairs on the sidewalk for customers who want to soak up the sun or shoot the evening breeze; to hang out, feel cool, stare out at an open-air parking lot, and inhale car fumes. Every once in a while, the small public bus that looks as if it's just been walloped and mugged joins the procession circling the block and, just for a second, the eyes of two estranged worlds meet.

I moved to Saifi in 2000. It was not my first choice. In the mid-1990s, I needed a place of my own and I wanted to be close to where I work and hang out, so that I might avoid languishing in my car for the rest of my working life. At first I wanted to rent an apartment in Achrafieh, a district inhabited mostly by Christians at that time and adjacent to the *wasat*, which had managed to retain some of its charm. My boyfriend, who had lived in Beirut through part of the war, advised me that I should choose a more mixed neighborhood. I finally opted for Saifi. It was a five-minute walk from my work and I wouldn't have to worry about upkeep. When I took up residence there, most of the site was still under construction. I rented space in one of the finished buildings until my apartment was finally completed. Easier that way, I thought. The rats were constant companions in those early days. One evening, Raghida, who was picking me up for dinner, called me from the car to tell me there was a rat party in the rubble around my building. When I complained to management, they assured me that the rats know not to enter the premises. Why? Had Solidere put up a no-entry sign for their benefit, I asked?

I finally moved to my purchased apartment in 2001. For more than a decade, I could not open my windows except on Sundays because of the noise and dust. I couldn't set foot in my apartment before 6 p.m. either, because of drilling in nearby buildings. In December 2007, when Hezbollah and its Christian ally, the Free Patriotic Movement (al-Tayyar for short in Arabic), occupied Martyrs' Square and its surroundings two streets up from my place, it was the sweetest month. In the mornings, I would put my reading chair on the balcony overlooking the inner garden and drink my coffee. No drilling, no cars, no soot and debris, only the birds, the sky, and me. I secretly prayed for the standoff to last at least a few weeks. I finally packed up and left for Clemenceau, an old, mixed quarter, in 2015.

In the October 2019 protests, someone had the sense to hang a banner in Arabic announcing, "This is *wasat al-balad*, not Solidere," in a symbolic attempt to bury the moniker and the era that made it possible. Only time will tell if we finally reclaim the name for the center.

Watching the spectacle unfold over a thirty-year run has been quite the ride, in equal parts burlesque, outlandish, indecent; a kind of gliding behavioral experiment, unconstrained and sadistic. As if the gods had had enough of our cravings and addictions and decided to let loose every temptation imaginable, in the hope that we might finally gorge ourselves to death. And we did. We emerged into the light in 2019, a bewildered people awoken from a state of delirium, and we were aghast at what we had done. We shared videos, reports, statistics, about the sheer scale of the voracious consumption and the pillaging that proceeded unabated, with resistance only from a few stubborn spoilsports whose warnings in the end mattered not at all.

But in this Second Republic, I cannot allow Hariri alone to hog all the attention. Hezbollah also ought to take a bow. Because in Lebanese juxtapositions, it doesn't get better than Hariri and Hezbollah, so different and yet so emblematic are they of Lebanon's quandaries. The two, a self-made Sunni billionaire and a grassroots Shiite resistance, loomed over Lebanon from very early in the 1980s. A magnate with an army of courtiers and a party with an army of warriors. The self-styled dealmaker and the self-anointed liberators. The former Saudi-made, the latter backed by Iran. The former very prickly about his sect's waning heft, the latter glaringly satisfied with the ascendance of theirs. The former sold on peace with Israel and its supposed windfalls, the latter wedded to the case for war and its supposed windfalls. But in essential ways—essential for the country, that is—they are cohorts of a sort. Both larger than Lebanon and larger than life. Both contemptuous of the state and with ambitions whose very success depends on the creation of parallel realms. Both with hordes of acolytes, followers, and hangers-on for whom nuance is a conspiracy and criticism treason itself. And both with a mass of enemies who attribute to them the same unforgiveable sin: sacrificing the whole in the service of one.

Neither one liked or trusted the other: different sensibilities and sectarian identities. But from 1992 to 2005, in the time of supposed calm, resistance, and plenty, Syria could easily chaperone the two. It was now master of the land, so to speak. For our neighbor and its president Hafez Assad, the moment was particularly sweet. A catchphrase of his, which decorated many a banner after 1990, captured the sentiment: "One people, two countries." It wasn't an unreasonable declaration on the face of it. It spoke plainly to the affinities between Lebanon and Syria, which could have been one by the grace of geography, language, and history; which could have been part of a larger whole, or, at least, in harmony with it had we had our wish in 1920; had the British and French left the Fertile Crescent well alone. But it was not to be after World War I.

We Arabs are endlessly fascinated by what might have been: had Britain and France been less interested in us, had the Zionists opted for a destination other than Palestine; and—since I am already on a roll of fantastical "what ifs"—had the Ottoman Empire been permitted to organically cede the ground to its aspirational subjects; had we Arabs had our way in shaping our future, or at least a strong say in it. But what we do know is that for the better part of the last one hundred years, we have been unsettled peoples unable to repair or remedy a terribly ill-conceived colonial inheritance.

And so, Syrian tutelage over Lebanon, with regional and international blessings, would do rather nicely for Assad—all things considered. And he would rule over us, pretty much like he ruled over his people. Trusted underlings from his security apparatus would oversee the protectorate, making brazenly clear to us the character of it. A relatively neat division of labor promptly ensued. Hariri would take the economic reins, in a nod to him and his Saudi patrons, and Hezbollah would devote itself to resisting Israeli occupation in the south. Lebanon's other political players would switch roles and positions, depending on circumstance and Syrian interests at the time. It all went swimmingly for a while. Assad was a brilliant puppeteer and Lebanese courtiers were such natural-born puppets. By 2000, both the prime minister and the resistance had succeeded: he curated the economy and they kicked out the Israelis. The only difference being that Hariri was now awash with muck, while Hezbollah had pretty much escaped from the stink of the Lebanese swamp.

When Hafez Assad passed away in 2000, *Pax Syriana* began to fray under Bashar, the son. He was green, less practiced than his father, less subtle. Lebanon's political class chafed from the rough treatment and began to entertain dangerous ideas. It was even whispered that the Sheikh was plotting to replace the Assads with a more amenable Alawite regime. In 2005, the arrangement finally unraveled and the Second Republic experienced a major jolt: Hariri was assassinated and Bashar subsequently lost his Lebanese concession. Hezbollah, robbed of the Syrian shield, unwisely jumped into Lebanon's political morass. Unsurprisingly, it quickly became "one of the boys" and watched itself grow increasingly petty and small. It's been fifteen years since, a little longer than Hariri's own run. A war with Israel in 2006, a major showdown in Beirut in 2008, several minor ones thereafter, and here we all are with the Second Republic—bankrupt, paralyzed, and defunct, and the Party of God unavoidably implicated in it all.

Such is the polarizing force of Hariri and Hezbollah that it has been convenient for the country to blame its ills on one or the other, when they are actually both guilty, much like the severe symptoms of a debilitating malady. I've always seen him and them more as innovators than inventors. Each, in their own special way, would bludgeon a conveniently savaged country, and thrive, along with a cheering political and financial chorus, in the myriad breaches. They did so, not because they didn't know any better or had no other choice or were coerced, but simply because this kind of Lebanon would do very nicely for them. It's frankly one for the books that the late prime minister was the showman who set the Second Republic on its catastrophic trajectory, and Hezbollah is the caretaker at the end of the journey trying to bring it safely to shore. The irony is that while neither had any patience or regard for the state, had it not been the way it is, neither would have found such a privileged place in its sun.

When opponents want to bash Hezbollah, they call it names: usurper, interloper, agent of Iran, shady, radical, murderous, a militant state within a state. . . . The names are meant to single the party out as a predator, an outlier, an anomaly. When Hariri's opponents want to bash him, they call him names: usurper, interloper, a tool of the West and of Saudi Arabia and Israel, boorish, a whale gobbling up everything in his way, a venal man who presided over a parallel state. The names are meant to single him out as a predator, an outlier, an anomaly.

To be fair to the pair, in their disdain for the Republic and encroachment on its powers, they have upheld a time-honored Lebanese elite tradition—in their loyalty and deference to outside patrons as well. But what gave Hariri and Hezbollah such extraordinary sway and impact in the postwar period was the sheer magnitude of their arsenal and the audacity with which they deployed it in a much-diminished Lebanon. From the outset, they were conquerors, and they both had the means to sweep a devastated country palpably weaker than both.

For Hariri, to rule meant that everyone whose signature and support he needed had to be the beneficiary of his largesse: presidents, parliamentarians, ministers, civil servants, professionals, professors, newspaper publishers, TV station owners, journalists, thought leaders, unionists, security bigwigs, judges. . . . During his tenure, it is said the lawmakers' favorite word was no. Hariri would present them with a plan, they would say no, he would turn on the money tap—and lo and behold the rubber stamp was produced and the scheme was approved. In Hariri mode, sectarian bosses became moguls, their families became financial powerhouses, their business interests widespread and diverse. Newspaper publishers upgraded their personal lifestyles. Hitherto blue-chip economists, lawyers, engineers, architects, and columnists were charmed, forming the Sheikh's inner circles and outer flanks. A perpetual circular motion of obstruction and bribery very soon became obvious. In a particularly reckless innovation, Hariri would even have his handlers and controllers in Syria on his payroll. In this labyrinth of his, there would be few exceptions: Hezbollah, notably, one of them. None of what I have just shared was ever a secret. Lebanon was abuzz with the extortionate sums exchanging hands. Stories flowed freely about the Haririan pattern. There is no other way to run the place, his defenders protested; there is no surer way to run it into the ground, his critics warned.

"Karkhana" is a special word in Lebanon. Around it, enemies rally, debates come to a halt, disagreement ends. In its original meaning, silk mill, the word was a plain Jane, dowdy even in sound. Its current bawdy meaning—bordello—was woven in a time of famine. When our mountains starved in 1916, the hungry women sheltering in the Karkhanas would prostitute themselves for calories. The word would thus be shorn of its old respectable definition and forced into its new debased identity. Thereafter, through the decades, it would be the description of choice for Lebanon's children when referring to the mother country in jest or in disgust. Which perhaps might explain why Hariri was incensed that some of us were offended when he did exactly what every john has done in the Lebanese Karkhana, except more generously.

I watched again recently Omar Amiralay's 2000 documentary about Hariri, *The Man with the Golden Soles*. There is a particularly amusing moment when the big man objects strenuously to the accusation that he entered politics by deploying his monetary might. Eight years into a deliberate and ostentatious display of financial muscle beyond anything to which any Lebanese had ever been tempted to succumb, you wonder what he could have meant? Then he went on to remind Amiralay that he was very generous to students, schools, universities, and hospitals long before he became prime minister. I paused the video for a second. Did he not know that we knew that he was angling for the job since 1982? Could he genuinely not tell the difference between charity and kickback? Or now that he had arrived and become "Mr. Lebanon" (a tasteless label if there ever was one), he was irate that his devotees, no less than his antagonists, still couldn't see beyond his cash. Rather like the female residents of Karkhanas who couldn't see beyond a suitor's banknotes, perhaps? I don't know. I would tick all of the above.

For me, Hariri's story with postwar Lebanon, even from its very early pages in the 1980s, has been rather straightforward—what he believed, what he wanted, what he was willing to do to get it, and what he finally achieved. The man was not particularly known for his subtlety. That wouldn't have suited his shock and awe tactics.

It certainly wouldn't have suited his own idea of himself: builder, savior, hero, and in that order for him, I would guess. Judging by Hariri's own words and actions, he most probably thought that if prewar Lebanon's ruling class sorely needed anyone, it would have to be him, a ringmaster orchestrating the team effort. So, what better improvement on the old Lebanon than him at the center of the now shattered one, because who else would be able to restore it to its erstwhile role doing what it has always done best: financial transit lounge, deal broker, and playground? But now with a manifestly Haririan flair for the spectacular.

It all reads like a scandal, but it wasn't. Not back then. Not for many, even for those who didn't much like Hariri or his epoch. Initially, I was mystified. Only from scattered liberal and leftist voices came the genuine protests and warnings about the meaning of it all. But I soon discovered two striking oddities, two distinct attitudes that let in the sun: a bizarrely resolute faith in our invincibility, our imperviousness to consequence no matter the wrong, and a smug fatalism about our irredeemableness, our incurability. This in a people whose modern history is a chronicle of pain, wasted opportunities, and loss. Often the punch line used by each attitude is the same: *Haida Libnain.* "This is Lebanon." When we are particularly pleased with ourselves—which is almost always—we sing the two words with a smirk, eyebrows lifting ever so slightly, head jerking gently sideways and backward to bring home the miracle. When we are confronted with our manifold sins—which is almost always—the voice drops sharply as the palm, open and up, rises barely a couple of inches to end the discussion before the accuser manages to land a point. As in, "This is who we are." This is our nature, our character, our destiny, our predicament as a half-serious country housing a half-baked people. As in, there is no room here for right and wrong, good and bad, except for tourists, for those who left. How that has ever squared in these people's minds, with their fury when, say, Hezbollah dismisses Lebanon with similar reasoning, is not entirely clear, most of all to them.

There you have it: *Haida Libnain* to reassure ourselves that we can indulge our avarice, our whims, our worst instincts, and defy the odds *ad infinitum*; and *Haida Libnain*, to shoo away with the back of our hand the proposition that Lebanon could be anything other than what it is and has always been. This is why *Harirism* was sure to outlive the man.

Recently, I have taken to singing the catchphrase to my friends. With a self-satisfied lilt for the boasting, or in a low voice for "it is what it is." We snigger as we slap our knees. And when I say we, I have a certain profile in mind. In fairness to Hariri, I cannot end this portrait of him without acknowledging a debt. Because, perhaps without even meaning to, he laid bare a truth about my circle, the so-called beau monde, aka the *haute bourgeoisie* and its appendages. Agog at the sheer nerve and flamboyance of the man and his era, we, practically in unison, dubbed it the Haririan Miracle and him Papa Noël, even though many of us privately couldn't stand the sight of him. Hariri pulled it off. He exposed the pretensions and flattened the false differences in this universe of privilege: between old money and new, between the nose-holding aristocracy and cigar-chomping parvenus, between the scions of traditional political houses and loud upstarts snapping at their heels, godfathers and bankers in suits, towering newspaper publishers and hustling arriviste writers, leftist armchair chin-scratchers and rightist firebrands.

You would have thought that, after fifteen years of carnage, Lebanon's patricians and guardians might have indulged in a bit of sobriety and introspection; that they might have seen a rare opportunity for reform in a severely damaged polity ripe for a rethink. If we had really wanted to, we could have built ourselves a more dynamic consociational democracy, a stronger civil state, and a more sustainable and vibrant political economy, as we could have done before the war. No ailment of ours was ever incurable, no weakness insurmountable. Instead, our warlords were handed the keys to the house and told to mind it some. "We had to buy civil peace with money," Hariri famously said.[5] His kind of peace, yes—for his kind of Lebanon. And we went along because it was the easier route; because we were sure that we would get away with it; that, no matter how crude our fault lines and senseless our greed, we would never be abandoned. That was only partly the Haririan effect on us, the rest arose from that gut certainty of ours that Lebanon is just too important to be forsaken by the Arab world, Europe, the planet. Because—all together with a lilt now—*Haida Libnain*.

"I am at peace with myself," Hariri declared to Amiralay at one point. Would that the stars were at peace with him. In the end, this tragic man would die three deaths. The first, physically shattering, in front of the St. Georges Hotel, where his motorcade was blown up and his statue now stands. The second a symbolic one, in the eerily barren and ghostly *wasat al-balad* (Solidere) where he now lies. The third in the collapse of the Second Republic that carries his signature.

The curtain rises with Hariri and falls with Hezbollah. What now? A country in disarray, a cast of characters in disbelief. In 1992, they all walked tall and mighty; by 2019, they're either dead or a different-sized midget. I do not know whether, for the Party of God, this quagmire is a prize or a curse. It's not a happy world that watches, nor a peaceful Levant that cradles, nor a century inclined to offering clues, let alone answers. The general sense is that the system and the movement are joined at the hip, sink or swim. You couldn't say that about any other political party without being laughed out of the room.

Hezbollah is just that big and Lebanon this puny.

That was the thing about Hariri *père*. Such an ill fit. Too big and too much in a country that is feather light and pint-sized. Look at what happened to him. Look at what happened to Lebanon. Is it not more so the case with Hezbollah? Such serious folk in such a frivolous country. But then how do you wish away enemies like Israel lurking on your doorstep? And yet, are fragile countries like ours meant to carry the burden of regional conflicts like the Israeli-Palestinian and Israeli-Iranian ones? Jordan and Egypt may not have prospered in the warmth of peace, but has Lebanon or Syria in the freeze of war?

Does this not make it plain that the sickness is partly within?

Is our failed Lebanon not making it that much easier for Israel to leave us thrashing in the wind, even as the resistance holds tight to its guns? The south is free, it is true—a great feat. Deterrence is essential. That cannot be denied. And the army is very weak by the will of the US and Israel, it is clear. But in whose scrawny dictionary is deterrence only about borders, missiles, and Kalashnikovs? How exactly is deterrence served by Hezbollah's degrading entanglement in Lebanese politics and protection of a band of thieves? How exactly does deterrence play in a sectarian bog like Lebanon, where the loot is about the only thing upon which our mafias are willing to agree? And yet, is it not a fact that were it not for a state long made impotent by its elites, Hezbollah, if it were to even exist in the first place, would be a much smaller and blander version of its current self? Would this not be the fate of all the Mini-Mes sniping at it or riding on its coattails?

This never-ending debate, at its most earnest and civilized here, has been going on for the past fifteen years. But down in Lebanon's political gutter, the repercussions of this quarrel are existential. Its enemies simply can't countenance the Shiite Party having such sway in Lebanon; its followers can't imagine a Lebanon without the party and its sway. All while both sides tear at the country themselves. They are all like demented children scrambling for their mother's favor even as they connive in beating her to a pulp.

The truth is, it was never going to be easy for Hezbollah. Shiite, Islamist, and Iranian constitute a red cape to a bull in Lebanon. For the Maronites and Sunnis, the two main curators of Greater Lebanon, which the French pulled together in 1920, the Shiites were never quite meant to come into their own as a sect. Nothing personal, just the lot of junior partners, of the third wheel. A matter of perspective, a question of habit. But the Shiites did come into their own, through diaspora, education, and war, pretty much in that order. You hear it quoted often among Shiite families, and certainly among mine: the migration to the city or to the world, the hard toil, the obsessive focus on education, the children who make it and lift entire clans. I trace it in that relatively short line between Umm Ali, my paternal grandmother, for whom the written word was foreign; my paternal grandfather, Abu Ali, whose own education stopped at the age of eleven; to my father, firstborn, who went to New York in 1950 on a one-year state scholarship to study aeronautical engineering, worked and paid his way through the remaining university years and returned in 1954 an engineer. With each sibling, the climb becomes easier, and for their children even more so, until the significance of the leap fades and is thereafter recounted as a "once upon-a-time."

It was a form of agitation, of course. The quiet kind that creeps up on history and nudges it toward a different shape until the time comes when it is, in parts, unrecognizable. Gradually, the old crowd had to move over a tad. Except in politics, where transitions tend to cause loud disruptions. There was never much love lost between upwardly mobile Shiites of the mid-century and their feudal lords. The former naturally wanted a more faithful reflection of their swelling expectations and rank; the latter, outmoded and outperformed, were inevitably losing control. The supposedly secular parties that had surged with independence and aged badly by the end of the 1960s fared no better for these aspiring Lebanese, or every other Arab. And so, they would turn to figures like Imam Musa al-Sadr, a cleric uniquely attuned to the changing tides. Iranian born but with deep familial ties to the south and a lineage that trumped passports, he came to Lebanon on the invitation of the son of Sayyid Abdul Hussein Sharaf al-Din, Tyre's Shiite scholar, who had passed away in 1957. The late Sayyid was keen to have Imam al-Sadr succeed him, and so it came to pass in 1959.

Like all trailblazers, al-Sadr was perfect for the opportunity that presented itself in 1975. History walking on legs is how one Shiite commentator described him.[6] If the Lebanese sect was finally ready to wield its power, al-Sadr was going to be the best man for the job. He combined good looks and charisma with political guile and populist appeal, religious venerability and an apparently tolerant outlook. He could draw in the different strands of his community, while confidently interfacing with other sects, playing the regional stage and rousing the grassroots. By the time I caught a glimpse of him in Amman, he had become Lebanese Shiites' torchbearer, his Amal Movement their party and militia. My parents had a dinner party for him during his stay in Amman. I sat discreetly on the stairs and watched as he entered. Quite the sight. Impossibly tall and magnificent in his robe and black turban. My mother remembers she cooked Jordanian Mansaf* for the dinner guests.

Soon after, he disappeared forever on a trip to Libya. Since that day in 1978, we Lebanese have had ourselves another set of gripping "what ifs." Certainly the biggest is how might have the Shiite community chosen to fill its seat at the table had al-Sadr not disappeared. But with or without him, at least we know this: the Shiite sect had to do quite a bit of persuading to have that seat in the first place. And it would take violence to do so. There was no Shiite exceptionalism in this path. That's how the Maronites and Sunnis had improved their own positions; the former in the clashes of 1840 and 1861, the latter in those of 1958.

All the same, annoyance, especially among the ruling cliques, was understandable. Nobody in politics likes to share. Besides, Shiite swagger after the war was bound to be irritating. They had already started sensing that they had won. So, every perceived Shiite audacity, major and trifling, was aired. The influx of money from Africa, the screaming status symbols that declared membership among the privileged. A sense of confidence and self-satisfaction that goaded you to look twice. "All in the goddamned cigar, innit?" a Shiite journalist friend of mine blared half-jokingly back in the early 1990s. "Have you seen a cigar longer than that brother of a whore they puff on—ANYWHERE?" These winners of the war would rattle even sections of their own sect: the smart, urbanized, secular Shiites at ease in their newfound milieu. They had already made it in previous decades, and the mantle, they felt, was rightfully theirs to inher-

---

*A lamb, rice, and dried and fermented sheep or goat milk dish.

it from the teetering feudal families. But Amal and Hezbollah made a mockery of their plans. If they wanted a role, they would have to thrive in the care of the sect's new gatekeepers, or not at all. Those who opted out would come to be known as the "alternative Shiites," or the "white Shiites"; in the parlance of Hezbollah and its circles, "the Shiites of embassies," as in agents of the West, traitors to the resistance, enemies of their sect.

Not that these same Shiites were ever unaffected by sectarian allergies well before the fratricide. Much like city folk everywhere, a mixture of Beiruti Christians and Sunnis were not happy with the growing presence of Shiites in their midst. The sect was urbanizing and populating different locales in Beirut, like Hai Illija (literally the "neighborhood of those who came"), and the mixed and middle-class Ras al-Nabe' and Nweiri, where my own paternal grandparents lived from the 1930s to the 1960s. The building where they rented was called the building of el-mtewleh,* a pejorative name for Shiites.

As I sit back remembering the stories shared through the years, one told to me by my cousin Hanan al-Shaykh, the novelist, sticks out. At a luncheon in the mid-1970s with her husband Fouad Ma'louf, his family, and friends, she was asked by one of Lebanon's star architects—a cosmopolitan to his bones, a sophisticate through and through—if she was from the al-Shaykhs of Beirut. No, we're from the south, she said. At which he delightedly dropped his gavel in mock judgment: "Ah, you are the jalab of Beirut" (the "riffraff" of the city). Truth be told, such jabs are lobbed in every direction, each nursing its own special grievance. There isn't a group that has been spared. This is a Lebanon of zawareeb (alleyways), where sometimes you feel your alley is your own little island. Only a couple of years ago at a party, an acquaintance asked me if I had moved from my apartment in Saifi. I said I had, to Clemenceau. "Oh, yeah," he winked. "I was at a luncheon there a few days ago

---

*The colloquial of Muta'wilah. It is said the Mamluks bestowed it on Shiites, in reference to their allegiance to Ali, the cousin of the Prophet Mohammad, and Ahl al-Beit, the house of the Prophet.

and they were mentioning that it looks like Shiites are moving more and more to the area." From what I gather, I am the fifth in the deluge of six families.

Par for the course all this, without Hezbollah. But in its shadow, in this hopelessly fractured slither on the shores of the East Mediterranean, we suddenly find ourselves in a pickle. Without the Party of God, so the logic goes, our problems are manageable. With it, a delicate balance tips into a hostile takeover.

It was never going to be easy for Hezbollah. Not that it ever cared much, as long as there was no actual threat to its carte blanche, inside Lebanon and out. But by now, when the so-called Lebanese experiment is in desperate need of yet another major makeover, the question must be asked: as the movement huddles to consider its options (and therefore ours) what propositions are tickling or harassing its imagination? That is, if it still has one.

It's one hundred years since the birth of Greater Lebanon, thirty years into its second incarnation. As we await the third, our prospects as a people have been reduced to a series of dismal scenarios. A much shorter span of this sorry history would have been infinitely more merciful on us, perhaps offering endings far better than our current nightmares.

But then—all together now, in that deep voice—*Haida Libnain.*

August 9, 2020.

Such are the times that I am compelled to return to this space with an afterword, weeks after I had sealed it with the four asterisks above.

On foot, yesterday at 9:30 a.m., I surveyed Mar Mikhael on the edge of *wasat al-balad* as smoldering shards of memory and life. August 4, the Port of Beirut belches fires from hell and the blast and furious sound waves rip through the eastern wings of the city. The Port, Mar Mikhael, Gemmayzeh, and the torso of Achrafieh that terrace the near hills hang this Saturday as landscapes of ruin. Buildings, friends' houses, my niece's; hangouts of the day and night; those who have died, those hospitalized, those picking up the pieces, and those who are done. Three hundred thousand people, they estimate, are without shelter, thousands more without windows and front doors, electricity and walls, water and hope.

I have come full circle and, it occurs to me, so has Beirut, twenty-nine years after that evening ride through *al-wasat* with Riad. As I walk the streets this time with my friend Rabih taking photos of heartbreak, I recall that coffin maker in his tiny atelier.

Rain drops onto windows. Very unusual in this city in August. Are the heavens shedding a tear or two for us?

That night in 1991, it was the tragedy of others that I beheld; today it is mine. Ours. Who would have thought? I mourn Beirut as a Beiruti. Finally!

CHAPTER 8

The Lived Moment

You return to that earlier time armed with the present, and no matter how dark that world was, you do not leave it unlit. You take your adult self with you. It is not to be a reliving, but a rewitnessing.

—Warlight Nathaniel Williams

I would like to say that my decision in 1991 to move to Lebanon was a mistake. Because it was. But then I never left, so I won't say it. At the beginning, Beirut was simply the answer to one incessant question: where to go and remain close? To origins, to intensely familiar surroundings and sentiments that offer continuums, however frail. I also wanted to be witness to a wrecked country as it reconstituted itself—or not, as it turned out. I thought it mildly interesting that we both were starting anew. I was eager to explore, to get closer to a birthplace heretofore unknown to me outside of research papers, books, and other people's memories.

And then there's that special quality to Beirut among Arab metropolises: it leaves you, as an Arab woman, single or married, alone, without losing sight of, or interest in, you. Here, in a wee cosmopolitan Beirut, no more than a few neighborhoods, you can pretend to live freely without fearing for yourself in the big bad world. It's just the particular groove of the place as history composed it. The laws and customs of the land are otherwise inclined. Personal status laws are still presided over by men of the turban and cloth. Patriarchy and misogyny have little to worry about here. On every international rating, Lebanon is near the bottom of the rung. But I roam, we roam, as if unaffected and exempt, in an existential free zone. And we can pretend to be free, because this part of Beirut pretends it is rather well. More often than not, its theaters, literary salons, clubs, art galleries, dress codes, and relationships, can test, explore, and massage boundaries with some confidence and with little fear of censure. Beirut in this way is a live and let live city. It makes Lebanon seem generous. It certainly felt that way to me as I strove to grasp the outré habits of the country.

I have lived in Beirut longer than I have lived anywhere else so far—thirty years. It's quite something to be an experienced practitioner in the art of Lebanese living. It's also nothing. My mood is the arbiter. Sometimes I ask myself, What have I done? Why did I choose this place? Why am I still here? Other times, I am a veritable Beiruti, the years behind me the raw material of this story that I now type.

At first, it was an immersion. Whether it was temporary or not, I didn't know. Lebanon was complicated, coy, crushed, and about to be put back together again, my assumption went. So, my instinct was to glide, the better to find my way in the boscage. I went to see Ghassan Tueni, the publisher of the leading daily *An-Nahar* and many other things beside—editor-in-chief, savant, diplomat, politician, wordsmith, savage wit, man of the world, night owl, lover of Christian icons, and the Greek Orthodox Church. He was also a very close friend of my father's since their SSNP days in the 1950s. Abu Fadi, who was a small shareholder in *An-Nahar*, told me that Tueni was contemplating a shakeup of his broadsheet, which was a pale, exhausted, much poorer copy of its original self. He had learned I was in town and wanted to meet. I had crossed paths with Amou (uncle) Ghassan only once before. I was a student in the US when he came visiting in Amman, and, later on, I just never sought him out.

That first meeting in Beirut, soon after my arrival, he made me wait for two hours in his personal secretary's office. I could have walked out, but I decided to be curious. When I was called in, through the haze of smoke, I saw my friend Malek and a couple of other young men. The two gentlemen left, Malek stayed. Amou Ghassan was rather abrupt, asking, almost as I began to sit, what he could do for me. I returned the favor, telling him he could do nothing for me; I didn't ask for the meeting, he did, so, the more appropriate question was what could I do for him? Malek turned to him and chuckled: "Think hard before your next move." We quickly settled into somewhat friendlier small talk. I don't know why Amou Ghassan had been curt. He always denied the charge when I teased him about it. I suspect he might have wanted to test my mettle, which he was fond of doing to others. Or it was to put me in my place, before I developed any silly ideas about favoritism because of family friendship. Or maybe this was his way of softening me up for his legendary charm offensive. Whatever the reason, we became friends, working together for two years on personal and newspaper projects. Years later, well after I had left for other endeavors, he would reach out from time to time with an idea, and we would pick at it until it gradually grew very old and tired.

I open with Amou Ghassan because this is how Beirut opened up to me. But there is more. I always saw him as an archetype, a personification of the myriad gifts and flaws of the world to which he and I belong. I am dragging him into *This Arab Life*, although I know it's not a role he would have liked to play. I would have rather not put him on the stage at all, but I simply can't write about Beirut without him in it. If this reads like an apology, first and foremost to Amou Ghassan, then let it be so.

To float in the orbit of Tueni was to hover in a fast-fading demesne whose inhabitants were hanging on to for dear life, one of fantastical tales, antiquated dreams, and stubborn hope that the postwar republic might somehow be an improvement on the prewar one. None of them was naïve or stupid or clueless or Panglossian, least of all Tueni, but they all had the notion that they could discreetly transform what they knew to be inauspicious beginnings into more reassuring results. A sentiment taken very much to heart by that upper tier of society that was reconciled to the epoch of Hariri. Their method was to whisper in a very small group of confidantes, cajoling, persuading, sweet-talking the powers-that-be behind closed doors, away from the public eye. It was more effective, they argued, but, in reality, public pressure or opposition couldn't possibly be their path because they had accepted the way things were; they had fallen in line.

These people were young and old, men and women, natives and returnees. They hailed from different sects, schools of thought, and professions. They were not necessarily friends, but through coincidence, work, and common friendships, inhabited Amou Ghassan's realm. Among the group were journalists and editors, lawyers and professors, would-be politicians and retired statesmen, old companions from this misadventure and that, the odd economist and businessman, the inevitable relative and sycophant. *The League of Lebanese Could Haves and Should Haves*, I called them, because practically every political conversation of theirs was a retrospection cloaked in *kan fina* and *kan lezem* (we could have, we should have).

I met these gentlefolk mostly at Amou Ghassan's house up in Beit Meri. At dinner parties, we would usually be no more than twenty. Sunday lunches were a ritual and more intimate. We would gather in the main living room at the bottom of the stairs, or the upper and lower terrace by the pool, depending on the number and the season. In a setting modern and comfortable, austere yet ornate, there would be a low hum of jolly chatter. Tueni would hold court. He would be fascinating, punctuating impeccably constructed analyses with delicious personal anecdotes. He knew much of what transpired at the highest level of politics and all the players. He had been, almost from the start, not at the heart of power, as was always his desire, but close enough to have stories to tell. His mind was partial to Gordian knots, shadows, cliffhangers, and double entendres; his sentiments were much easier to fathom. He rejoiced in the swing of the much younger Lebanon of the '40s, '50s, and '60s; in the fact that he was one of its illustrious sons when it was at its most elegant and worldly and compelling. He even reveled in its dramas, much like he reveled in his own: Lebanon, a fabulous but delicate nation abused every which way by unscrupulous forces; Amou Ghassan, a heroic but stoic soul tested by a cruel fate and suffering unspeakable hurt. It made of him an ardent believer in the gallantry of Lebanon—*nay* (as he would have said) in the sacredness of it—and beyond that in the Almighty himself. An unwavering belief in God and country that anchored him, laced his musings, and accessorized his walls in Beit Meri, a choreography of Lebanese landscapes and religious icons.

Tueni was unique among his peers; an intellectual tour de force and a man of action, a lettered gladiator, and striving politician. And always the newspaper man; in his own mind probably a Ben Bradlee and Katherine Graham composite. Floating in his universe, for me, was a form of multidisciplinary field research. An education, really. I had lucked out. There were few sages in Lebanon to match Tueni. Through him I could trace the unraveling of a nation that had started out with magnificent pretentions in 1943, the year of independence, and was ending in heartbreak. What better view was there for me, a mere spectator at that point, of a troupe of paladins scrambling to gather the smashed pieces of their faith in the old place in order to cheer on, with a clean conscience, the new one? He didn't see it that way, but I did, paradoxically, in part thanks to him.

A friend dear to Tueni and me once said of the man: "He could have been great, but he settled for interesting." It could have easily been his epitaph. A fair verdict perhaps, but one born out of the disappointment that love and its inexorable expectations often engender. I've written before about how Lebanon can be blinding that way; a capricious creature given to leaving in the wake of its many love affairs a trail of lovers betraying their better selves for its pleasure. Amou Ghassan was one of them. "The wars of others on our land" is his famous coinage. He meant it as an argument, not an excuse, but it survives solely as the latter. His premise, in very rough terms, was that Lebanon could have managed its difficulties and would have been spared the violence of its contemporary history were it not for foreigners using his country as proxy to wage wars and settle scores. It's a contention that thrives as folklore, even though it has died a million deaths in the real world where we mere mortals live. And those who have killed it are none other than the Lebanese themselves. In Tueni, the contention that Lebanon is more victim than culprit, more heroine than villain, betrayed intent. In the end, all he wanted to do was tinker, maybe creatively, maybe even boldly for some, including him, but tinkering is just not the stuff of greatness. In his dialectics on Lebanon, there was no greater mismatch than that between his Herculean visions and the utter mess on the ground.

Other passions intruded as well. Tueni had truly wanted to be president. He was just ambitious that way. But he, a Greek Orthodox, could never be president in a state whose pinnacle of power was constitutionally reserved for a Maronite. This desire would be the curse of his life, trumping his better instincts, his better angels. So, he settled for playing second fiddle, at times to much lesser men than himself. I mention this because Tueni was not alone. Many Lebanese of similar caliber did the same: those *who could have and should have* but didn't.

In Amou Ghassan, I see the concessions of an older generation of doers and thinkers, whatever their ideologies and paths. I see it in me and mine, in my generation in Beirut, Damascus, Cairo, Amman. . . . For whatever reasons that motivated us—comfort, security, power, fear, delusion, or simply because we thought that it is what it is—all we wanted to do was tinker. But tinkering, however its virtues may be argued, is not the stuff of salvation either.

I would have liked to have known Amou Ghassan when Lebanon's allure and his were as much promise as pretention. When he and *An-Nahar* were all the rage, his pen by turns a sword and a gavel, the interplay between the cunning operator and august journalist a beguiling dance. But the difference in age between us would have us meet in the 1990s instead, when neither Lebanon nor he could muster much of a persuasive second act. For him, the past—thrilling, fully lived, Byzantine, in far too many parts tragic, in some rueful—suggested self-reflections and farewells. It was a past full of stains from every stopover and detour, none more visible than the defunct May 17, 1983, Israeli-Lebanese agreement that Tueni helped negotiate as special advisor to President Amin Gemayel. The pact, a withdrawal deal in name, a bilateral peace treaty in effect, would tear at Lebanese reputations. The tarnish on Tueni never quite wore off with time, his own historical stand against Israel presenting the saddest twist in the unedifying situation. He always revisited history with moxie and panache, not so 1983. At least, not with me. I gather from his writings, and from his friends, that he imagined Lebanon in this specific instance as in all others, a player in its own destiny, and not just a helpless pawn. I don't know if friends like Palestinian-American scholars Walid Khalidi and Edward Said, whom I used to see in Beit Meri, ever sought enlightenment from Tueni on his role. In his private conversations with my father, I am told it brought him to tears.

Then there was *An-Nahar* postwar. Its readership was drastically down, its look dull. It was not alone in an ailing Fourth Estate desperate for a facelift and cash. Between Amou Ghassan and me, the topic did not sit well. The matter of money was always *the Hariri* in the room, as I once joked. When we fought about matters to do with Hariri, he would insist on the usefulness of strategic dissent and tactical endorsements. I would calmly call them copouts. At times, he would be furious with me, especially when it came to Solidere. I thought he conveniently cherry-picked his criticisms in his columns; he thought I was insensitive to the times and the necessity of compromise when the cards are few and the hand is weak. He would attack, and I would take it in stride, because, well, he was Amou Ghassan. When, in the early '90s, I worked with the novelist Elias Khoury on a documentary about Solidere, a project that never saw the light of day, Tueni was encouraging. I distinctly remember him telling me that he had privately been able to save a few historical buildings otherwise earmarked for destruction in Solidere's master plan. I never asked which ones.

The 1990s were, for Tueni, a restless decade. He said he wanted to reinvent *An-Nahar*. He never did. He sensed an opportunity in television. But he didn't know whether he should launch a program or an interview series. He eventually did a couple of television interviews, one with King Hussein, soon after the 1993 Oslo Accords, another with the Grand Ayatollah Mohammad Hussein Fadlallah, Lebanon's highly esteemed senior Shiite religious authority. There was so much to be done, Tueni felt, but there was pain and damage in him. His was a broken, smoke-filled heart. A daughter, Nayla, lost to the sweet hereafter in 1963 at the age of seven; a son, Makram, who followed her there at the age of twenty-one in 1987; and a wife, a poet, Nadia, who succumbed in 1983 at the age of forty-eight. They were everywhere in the hours of his day—in family photos, in fleeting ruminations and odes, in the womb of his garden in Beit Meri, where mother and daughter lie in eternal repose. He would often sit there in the shade of the trees, private anguish a burden too much, an aging *An-Nahar* in a bleak media landscape a drain all on its own. It seemed that postwar Lebanon was nudging him to the margins, even though he was still in his sixties. He was keen, but he was adrift.

Tueni would, for me, come to embody the malaise of the Lebanese elite, many of them keen to reflect and yet forget; to move on but remain attached to possibilities long dead; to revive their fortunes and concede hard-earned wisdom toward that end. In the Second Republic, they would simply tag along. Individual sparks may have ignited here and there, lighting up the drabness of institutions and the collective self. Individually, they may have amounted to something. Together, in spite of their best efforts and dearest hopes, they didn't amount to much. *An-Nahar* would manifest all this: a spiritless front page pulsing with the columns of Samir Kassir; lackluster coverage lent substance by the weekly intellectual supplement of Elias Khouri, a defector from rival *As-Safir*. Khouri would eventually leave, and Kassir would be killed by a bomb placed under his car in June 2005.

Gebran, Amou Ghassan's last surviving son, was also killed in 2005. On December 12, his car exploded as he was driving down from Beit Meri. He was the fourth to die in the wave of assassinations that started that year.

Amou Ghassan passed away in 2012. A couple of years before, a series of strokes had already transported him to a world that none of us could reach. My father would visit him regularly. I couldn't. The last time I saw him, we sat in his study. I talked, he stared. I touched his cheek, his eyes blurred with tears. His second wife, Chadia, and Abu Fadi told me the tears fell often.

Writing about the dead is a very delicate, thankless affair. A

Author's father (left) and Amou Ghassan, 1990s.

million and one portraits of a life are sure to emerge. In the end, you craft your own particular one, to the chagrin of many and the satisfaction of few. But then personal perspectives are all I offer in this book.

And have we not been a people keen and adrift? A short-sighted and grasping prewar elite, a blind-as-a-bat, and a greedy postwar one. A swarm of cocooners convinced that individual vitality made up for communal languor; that a singular flourish of the pen, the brush, the mind, the eye, the spirit, somehow sufficed. That since we were forbidden, under pain of one form of death or another, from collectively authoring another narrative for our country, we would each stitch together something for our own miniature dominions. We would insulate ourselves from the indignities that enveloped us while hiding our own. Has this not been the theme that binds all of us tinkerers?

And stitch I did upon arrival in Beirut in 1991. I had no choice. Barely months in, it became clear that the best way to live in the country was to divide my world into as many bubbles as I could manage, the better to navigate and experience the absurd: the political deformities of the country, its social incoherence, its insistence on speaking in tongues.

To a newcomer to the scene, on the ground, day-to-day, at first sight, Lebanon is a Hobbesian chaparral. Except it isn't. There are canons, conventions, etiquettes, maestros who author them, subordinates who impose them, sentries who protect them, and people who abide by them, happily or not. They're written nowhere, they might change for no apparent reason at all, and you can't learn them fast enough in order to get by and get on. Principles have expiration dates, subject to renewal, depending on the issue and the benefits attached to it. Prejudices are generally more difficult to barter away, but even those can go into hiding momentarily for the right price.

For us Lebanese, as individuals, the state is at once nonexistent and predatory. Its purpose, deep in its bowels, is to organize and finance sectarian clout and benefits, such as employment, promotions and other services, and to bless sectarian malfeasance everywhere else. The aim of every third functionary, it seems, is to personally fleece us however they can; ours is to disappear into the background and, when that's not possible, negotiate down the bribe. The confounding labyrinths of policies and laws are in fact immaterial, more opportunities for private profiteering than checks on wrongdoing and excess.

Every day, therefore, there are decisions to take. I have gathered here just a sample from my own circle of friends.

Do I bribe the electricity department official to stop my bill from spiking for no reason at all? Yes.

Do I bribe the head of payment collection (Caisse) at the municipality to abide by the ruling of the courts on the outrageous estimate of my company's rent? No.

Do I bribe the state auditor assigned to my long dormant, empty shell of a company to close it down so that I can transfer the shares of my partners to a newly formed one? Yes.

Do I bribe the responsible engineer in the municipality to paper over a structural change in my apartment, permission for which was not approved in the first place to allow for a bribe? Yes.

While renovating this apartment, do I bribe the gendarmes who keep visiting and placing a red mark on the apartment in order for me to pay them to lift it? Yes.

Do I pay, in cash, the inheritance tax office to avoid a punishing tax on my late husband's estate set too high to convince me to pay the bribe and close that file? Yes.

Do I pay the airport customs to let in a shipment for which they may set a prohibitive customs charge? Yes.

Do I bribe the traffic policeman to avoid a ticket? No.

Do I bribe the housing authority to issue the official deed for the office I own? Yes.

Before long, if you are well-to-do, or are lucky enough to have brothers or sisters or cousins or kissing cousins or buddies or fathers-in-law spread across the bureaucracy, you build yourself a network of intermediaries psychologically equipped and trained to deal with the madness. You find yourself complicit in the very machinery of corruption you fume about at the dinner table—a hypocrite, compelled to constantly feed a system you hate, because it refuses you the right to live any other way without a great cost to your sanity and health.

The state is itself quite poor and yet it's a golden goose to the high-ups. As foreign aid pours in mindlessly, debt piles up, and contracts both large and small are dispensed with sinister care. Crookedness is blatant, expected, accepted, serious, nebulous, and nearly impossible to prove with a real paper trail—at least not one accessible to the public. And even when, on the auspicious occasion that evidence is within reach, hardly a blip registers on the country's radar of shame. Journalists may investigate, newspapers may publish on the front page, TV stations may broadcast on the evening news, social media may disseminate with mockery and indignation, people may snigger and tsk-tsk, but then we all move on. The quest for data is like the search for the Holy Grail. And when you are fortunate enough to stumble upon it or find it after a hard day's work, you hold it in tiny, half-comprehensible bits of a puzzle, the remaining parts of which are strewn like grain in a field of sugarcane. An entire economy built on theft is rigged to fudge facts and numbers or drown them in a sinkhole of claims and counterclaims. The idea is to make hearsay possibly fact, and fact arguably hearsay. You would expect such obfuscation in the major files, where corruption thrives. Not so! The fog is actually designed to permeate every facet of everyday life.

It is up to you whether you are immune to or continuously pissed off by all this, but in case you have opted for the former, luckily the immunity doesn't have to be naturally achieved. Lebanon offers such easy access to antidepressants, hashish, and other send-offs, you would think it's a national policy to help people cope with the weirdness. You very quickly discover that, with or without immunity, you have methodically built yourself a cocoon, where you get to work, live, eat, drink, party with your friends and family, according to your own norms and rules in your own *res publica*. A confection of fantasies, facilities, and conceits pulled together by fixers, connections, and shortcuts, this cocoon, gradually grows into a permanent residence of a sort. Bizarrely, your world begins to expand and shrink at one and the same time. It expands because Lebanon's fast style becomes yours, if you so choose, and you convince yourself that it's all gratis. You get to do pretty much whatever you like, short of murder. Although, with contacts and traditional workarounds, courtesy of, say, your sectarian chieftain, even that might be forgiven. The kindness of Lebanon expands your horizons in many other essential ways. There is no penalty for ineptitude, for being caught with your hand in the piggy bank, or even for war crimes. In Lebanon, you might be insane, or an idiot, or on the run; scorned, laughed at one day, only to soar, high and mighty, the next; maybe as a cabinet minister, member of parliament, prime minister, president, or newly minted tycoon.

Your universe shrinks because its geographies and demographics dwindle. Boroughs outside your locale become travel destinations. Because of traffic, convenience, milieu, class, sect, and politics, you begin to nestle in your cocoon-cum-dominion, visiting other parts of the city as if they were other commonwealths. Slowly, only what happens in your immediate vicinity begins to matter. You start having a false sense of self-sufficiency, an autonomy unencumbered by circumstances and events, unless they impact you and yours in a very direct, glaringly visible way. Which tallies with the feelings that develop for the state itself whose relevance to your needs, your comforts, your routine, your sense of place, becomes negligible because it is actually negligible. You don't actively think about the strangeness of this existence, it just becomes one of the many odd facts that make up your world.

On December 12, 2007, my best friend Joye called me from Washington, DC, at around 2 p.m. Beirut time. She had just read about the assassination of Major General Francois Hajj, chief of operations in the Lebanese Army, and wanted to know if I was safe. Between 2005 and that day, Lebanon had witnessed a major war between Hezbollah and Israel, a three-month battle between the Lebanese Army and jihadist Fatah al-Islam in the Nahr al-Bared Palestinian camp in Tripoli, and eight assassinations. The dead included a prime minister, a member of parliament and former minister, a member of parliament and minister, a journalist, another journalist and member of parliament, two parliamentarians, and a one-time head of a political party. There were also three unsuccessful attempts against a minister, a journalist, and a senior officer in the Internal Security Service. In the meantime, we had a cabinet paralyzed by the resignations of the ministers of Hezbollah and al-Tayyar, its Maronite ally, and protests and sit-ins in *wasat al-balad* to bring down the government. I asked Joye where would she be if the US had experienced a war with Mexico that displaced millions in the south; a brutal battle between the army and a Christian fundamentalist militia in New Jersey that devastated the infrastructure of a town-sized compound; two assassinated senators; two assassinated *New York Times* journalists, one of them the editor-in-chief of the paper; two assassinated cabinet secretaries; an assassinated vice president; and year-long protests and sit-ins around Congress? She said she would be in a bunker somewhere. I told her that I was having lunch with Huda at the lovely

Balthus, just two streets down from the havoc. Beirutis coped during the war by following the pace and location of the street battle. This is exactly how we have lived in peacetime. The city, in this sense, never really transitioned, even as the violence ebbed into intermittent blows. I stayed at The Coral Beach Hotel in West Beirut for a month in 1980. I tasted wild nights at the hotel's Beach Comber or the Summerland's Mikano, dinner at Calvados, or on the balcony at a friend's, all the while mortar rounds playing in the background like side drums. As a guest, I thought the Lebanese unhinged. As a Beiruti, I still think us unhinged, but I have discovered that this is our way of looking after our wee selves in our wee worlds.

You don't plan it, you might not even want it, but before you know it your scope—the events that form and shape your days, the characters that fill them, the crucial relationship between you and what counts—has grown as small as your radius. The country offers itself up in pieces, so you take them, spruce them up and make them your abode. The rest you can simply ignore. Foreigners see a riddle and marvel at it. We Lebanese see rips and tears and weave them into a glorious illusion. This is how Lebanon comes alive only in fragments. Why its entirety is such a dim prospect and yet its parts can be so luminous: design, food, entrepreneurs, great doctors and architects, brilliant novelists and artists, magnificent landmarks, the eco-lodges hidden in the Barouk, Ehden, and Shouf. . . . All of these sparkling elements in the midst of a corrupt, filthy, sectarian, amoral, dysfunctional, reckless, careless, state. We perch in our very small, beautiful truths and come to believe that somehow we will escape the much bigger ugly one.

There are other ways in which your world shrinks in Lebanon. Since, finally, the twenty-first century laid bare the Arab people's visceral disdain for their regimes and the latter's mortal fear of their people, architectures of siege have arisen everywhere. Security barricades encircle embassies, UN buildings, ministries, parliament, politicians' houses, rendering Beirut a rodent maze. It is said that Beirutis have no easy access to over twenty percent of the city, now a busy collage of security zones. In some cases, this is to protect certain politicians from death; in most, it is to physically shield the government from the people whose very interests and concerns it's supposed to serve.

I live in one such area in Clemenceau. My neighbor, around the corner, is Walid Jumblatt, the Druze leader. The side street on which his house is located is protected by two checkpoints manned by his own men. Car access to my street is controlled as well by two security barriers. The guards are respectful, the mornings quiet, the nights silent. What more could I ask for in a city that is always screaming?

We have learned to live with the red and white barricades of Beirut the way we have with all other hurdles. Like traffic signs, they have grown invisible to the eye. The architecture of our rulers' dread of the hereafter has become the routine of our life here and now. Even more so today as we, masters and subjects, nervously watch our worlds of make-believe crumble and fret over the fallout and exit.

Postscript

I meant to show the few pages on Amou Ghassan to Abu Fadi, as soon as I was done. I wanted the reassurance of a nod. And if not, then the wisdom he might impart. But there are no more conversations to be had with Abu Fadi—not this kind, not the way we used to, since I first could make sense of an emotion or a thought, not in this life. He's gone. It's twelve days now. September 9, 2020.

This grief—this grief—I mean this type of grief. In the blink of eye, I am forever lost in a vast expanse of words, so many words, and flashbacks and tears and smiles. There is nowhere for me to go but back to the early hours of August 29, when I kissed his forehead for the last time, to when I was three and he was thirty-three; when I was fifteen and he was forty-five; when I was thirty and he was sixty; forty and seventy . . . Like that the clock keeps ticking backward, randomly picking up pieces of us. Because now that's all there is of him and me.

That's all I want to say.

I read again this morning what I wrote about Amou Ghassan. I couldn't judge it without Abu Fadi's counsel. If it's still here when you're reading this, then I will have taken the advice of my friends. If not, there probably will be little or no trace of him. It will be a different chapter and you wouldn't even know it.

Four parting words: I love you, Papa.

Author's father (left) and the author, 1985.

CHAPTER 9

What's Left

Historically, pandemics have forced humans to break with the past and imagine their world anew. This one is no different. It is a portal, a gateway between one world and the next. We can choose to walk through it, dragging the carcasses of our prejudice and hatred, our avarice, our data banks and dead ideas, our dead rivers and smoky skies behind us. Or we can walk through lightly, with little luggage, ready to imagine another world. And ready to fight for it.

—Arundhati Roy

Early every Sunday morning, I walk. The cars are few, the air is relatively free of soot, and el-Zaitouneh by the sea is 5 minutes away. But since COVID-19 and the lockdowns, I have taken to walking that *corniche* three times a week. If I turn the full circle of the inner road and a couple of the side streets on the reclaimed land that completes the bay, I get the 45 minutes of exercise I need. Solidere was supposed to turn at least part of this landfill into a park; it's still the desert though, bare roads and sidewalks, encircling dispersed structures and tracts of shrubs, gravel, and stone.

Two weeks after the Beirut port explosion, I walk as if I am the last person on earth. There is an all-pervading emptiness, with abandoned, mangled buildings, and only my shadow on the asphalt: for once, a *mise-en-scène* in keeping with the city's mood. It feels no different to walking amidst the devastations of Karantina, Mar Mikhael, Gemmayzeh, and Geitawi, the last of Beirut's old neighborhoods. Here, Bohemia had embraced the city's unwanted and harassed—Kurds, Syrians, Ethiopians, LGBTQ communities—much like it did the cool bars, artists, and quirks.

Every sight is a metaphor. Every small death of things speaks to a much larger one of what might have been. The center of Beirut is a ruin. The city is on its knees, and so is Lebanon. The pandemic has been very hard on us but not catastrophic. In a truly Lebanese twist of fate, though, it has crushed already sputtering street protests, giving the government much-needed respite. Accursed, an old favorite expression of ours, is bouncing about with renewed vigor. We feel we are damned. A cliché we casually tossed into a tired political discussion or a swift chat at the grocery store has become our mantra as we click shut the luggage on our way out.

Fires continue to erupt at the port. Smoke from burnt cooking oil and burning tires or similar hazards billows out, with little public explanation or investigation. It's a rare treat when a state's decrepitude exhibits such raw physicality. How will our congenital want of sweet miracles and narrow escapes crawl its way out of this wreckage? For now, at least, our temperament is in tune with our predicament.

As I wrap up, US dollar deposits have been illegally denied us by a bankrupt banking sector with political cover from the state and Central Bank, themselves bankrupt. The Lebanese lira becomes more worthless by the day, but the official peg remains 1,500 LBP to the US dollar. So, we have now four exchange rates. There is little value to our savings, and what's more, the judiciary has been unofficially instructed to derail any legal action by depositors. Our subsidized fuel is sold in trickles. We smuggle it to Syria, we hoard it to jack up the price, we cheat, we scream and punch each other in endless queues, and we pay. Publicly provided electricity has all but ceased and private generators just can't keep up. Darkness for the many, light for the few. Pharmacies and hospitals are running out of essential medicine and supplies. There is a black market for nearly everything. Those of us who have access to fresh US dollars manage well; those who don't are doomed.

We have no government, even when we do. Our parliament meets every once in a while to tick some boxes or to see if it might pass laws designed to protect the ruling gang against what's coming. An outcry ensues and, practically to a man, they feign innocence and outrage in solidarity with the populace. Our economic collapse is deemed one of the world's worst since the nineteenth century. We don't know how much the Central Bank has in foreign reserves, because Riad Salameh, the Central Bank governor, refuses to disclose the numbers, but we know we will run out very soon. The IMF says it won't come to the rescue without a forensic audit. The reigning cabal fears they won't last after it. And while the IMF might bring in precious cash and financial discipline, we know what its remedies will be, and the austerities they will impose. In the meantime, France, England, and Switzerland are investigating Salameh for money laundering and embezzlement. But he refuses to resign and those who could remove him are protecting him instead.

In any event, for all the hullabaloo, the system presides over us still intact, in control, and immovable. Its behavior grows more and more bizarre by the day, but it holds fast, its head deep in the sand. In our impotence, we have resorted to mockery. Tweets, posts, and video clips are constantly making the rounds. Every once in a while one appears with a distinct sting. "Look at the price of bread, the price of fuel, the price of gasoline," the man shouts at a TV reporter in one such clip. "We have missiles that can hit Israel, but we don't have suppositories to shove up our ass."

We curse with him and then we laugh.

It's December 2021. Like everywhere, it has been more than a year of masks, lockdowns, and warnings against hugging loved ones. But COVID has been surprising in the small gifts it has offered, along with the panic and grief it has unleashed. For the first time in nearly three decades, I took the road to places I never cared to know before, it was all so quiet and empty here. And I am stunned by how beautiful Lebanon remains in spite of it all. In spite of us. Little havens in Tyre and Ma'asser al-Shouf, in 'Ain Zhalta and 'Aqoura, toward Anfeh by the coast. . . . The companionship that comes with being grounded has been a blessing as well. All my life, I yearned for time with my father, who was forever on the move, even when he was in one place. Now, he gladly lunched with me on my balcony every few days, and the morning coffees on his and my mother's balcony became so wonderfully slow. It turned out to be a blissfully long farewell. And I finally understood for the first time what my Beiruti friends meant by the special mood of the civil war. The huddle in each other's homes, the camaraderie, with conversations and laughter piercing the eerily quiet days and evenings. The lightness of being that takes hold as if to snub the weight of life itself.

There is dismay, to be sure. Surrender as well. It's not a deep-seated fear of intimately familiar implosions, like sectarian violence or economic disintegration, that explains the white flag, but a new dread: that our truce with the chaos of Arab life is for the birds. The freak show wins. As we survey our own country, the Levant, the Fertile Crescent, and Arab territories beyond that grow ever more daunting in their blights, it seems wise to just call it quits. The implications are clear. We leave. Among my own friends and family, those who are staying are the ones who have nowhere to go, or are bound by work but have sent their families away, or have their careers behind them and can bolt in the event of total lawlessness. There are a few who are hanging on because they simply cannot bring themselves to let go.

But I sense something different in this season of escape. Those leaving are doing so for good, it seems. Unlike the generation of escapees during the civil war, many of whom left with the intention of returning with the return of peace, this fellowship of émigrés does not plan to come back to work or invest or build anything. They know the country is just not salvageable. For them, Lebanon, so long as its troubles remain bloodless, will very likely be only for family reunions and their children getting a taste of the old place.

I sense something new among the younger nomads as well. Their horizon has moved much closer to home. Europe and the US are out of reach, so as we crumble on this side of the Mediterranean and the Red Sea, it's destinations like the UAE they seek first. Stability, order, and good pay is freedom enough to an exhausted youth. The rise of such city-states may be instructive for us as we attempt to build our own, because it looks like that is what we are fast becoming. Or it may not. The future of the Fertile Crescent, as it continues to unfold in a mess of furious trends, is as yet unreadable.

The *New York Times* is entertained by the irony that those volunteering in the aftermath of the blast are none other than the youth filling up immigration applications.[1] But Levantine youth have been volunteering and leaving for decades. Theirs is the twin expression of love of country and despair at those running it. No irony there. And the apparent push and pull between commitment and flight is not solely the province of the young. There is, in fact, a deeper meaning to the actions of volunteers, philanthropists, charities, aid agencies, activists (of differing ages and incomes) who swoop down with brooms, cash, food, medical aid, hammers, and nails to the "ground zeros" of our lives, as we pack up. We are a people long conditioned by our regimes to pick up the pieces of whatever they themselves break, tend to the wounds they inflict, fill the vacuums they create. Descending on the port area is nothing more than a hyperextension of our mode of daily existence. Just look at the torn neighborhoods a year after the blast, many refurbished, fixed, and mended now. By us.

Ours, in the words of Assef Bayat, is "the art of presence" under impossibly difficult conditions. I might be taking liberties with his term; he most probably has in mind a less busy human collage. But for me, the beauty of this art of presence is its generous representation of the human spirit in distressed terrains, and the clarity with which it depicts the fraught relationship between *them* and *us*. We do our thing, they say, and you go about your business, hushed and head down. You do your thing, we say, and we go about our business, individually or in scattered duos, trios, or quartets, nudging the needle, securing victories, however small, and inducing concessions, however modest. We win reprieves and breathing room; they cede inches and keep their precious thrones. This arrangement is holding even though little else does. Hence our novel dread. In the place of the state, we have fiefdoms; in the place of a single master, a gang of them; in the place of the familiar tangle between ruler and ruled, hide and seek with faceless men.

In Beirut, volunteers have swarmed over decimated sections of the capital where there is no discernable trace of the state. The art of absence becomes one side of yet another juxtaposition. Two hundred people have lost their lives, 300,000 have lost their homes, 640 historic buildings have become vulnerable to the developers' bulldozers. But it's the Red Cross that evacuates the injured and the dead; activist app developers who digitize maps of the destruction; donors and volunteering architects and engineers who rebuild homes; child protection charities that care for the orphaned and the abused; the refugee assistance organizations that tend to the homeless.

This is our world: vast panoramas of absence and presence. It used to be that those in search of hope on our shores, including us Lebanese, would point to our art of presence as a sure sign of resistance and resilience. They were not wrong. But then, carried away by this lovely thought, they would start to insist that this was the Arab world's real story—all humanity and color and grit—the one that counted, maybe even the one that could ultimately triumph. And so the reasonable quest to illuminate a million small and disparate victories of the human will turns into an exercise in fantastical thinking.

I suspect few of us are interested in this kind of maudlin crocheting anymore. It's been a very hard decade on us, the apt finale to a very hard one hundred years. The lessons from 2011 have been particularly cruel for our youth. And theirs, of course, is the burden of enticing the future in a direction that may yet redeem this region. And how wonderful the opportunity, because they start with practically everything in pieces. What was once Greater Syria, what was once the state, what were once our cities, the cultures they spawned, the forces that honed the very shape of us, the stuff of our dreams and nightmares.

I don't know what we will make of these shreds of places and peoples and ideas. But somewhere in all this, surely there must be fragments of answers. It is true that this presence of ours, for all its inventiveness, doesn't do change *a la granda*. It's not meant to. Of all the realities that 2011 has revealed, this one has the luster and the toughness of a gemstone. And perhaps herein lies the sweetest paradox: We may have failed in sweeping change, but change has been sweeping all the same. The page is not blank by any means, but it is today unusually receptive to a rewrite.

Acknowledgments

I start this page, the way I start every morning, with a longing to have one last conversation with my father. I want to tell him, again, how blessed I am to be his flesh and blood, to have been the recipient of such love and kindness and generosity and wisdom. *This Arab Life* that I have had, in all its wondrousness, wouldn't have been possible without him.

My one consolation is the moments I have with my mother in repartee and remembrance.

The last three years have been quite the journey, all reflection and sorrow and ink, much of it in solitude. In crossing it, I have been unusually demanding of family and friends, many more than I would typically turn to for feedback and guidance. I reached out to them in different countries, from different generations, with stark differences in histories and outlooks. I needed resonance and perspective. And they did not disappoint.

All my gratitude goes to my family, Fadi, Raghida, Asma, Iman, Fares, Rawan, Bassel, Noor, Myra, Ali, and Lara for their love and support. I am especially grateful to Myra, Fares, Rawan, and Bassel for their meticulous notes and insights. Heartfelt thanks as well to my friends, Sami, Rabeh, Reem, Huda, Elie, Samar, Safwan, Hanan, Rula, Malek, Hala, Nour, Rabih, Sherif, Hazem, and Chris, all the keenest of readers. To Joye, soul mate and all-around nuisance in pushing me to beat down my doubts and write, a special "chapeau bas."

I am deeply indebted to Fawwaz Traboulsi, for so many years an inspiration from afar, recently a friend and mentor, for his invaluable critique. Equally so to Peter Harling for his sensitive counsel and incisive remarks.

I had every expectation that I would be thanking as well my dear friend Christopher Dickey for his extraordinary eye and deft annotations. But he left us in July 2020, before I was ready to share the early drafts, and my life and certainly this book are all the poorer in his absence.

I have been especially fortunate in my editors, Susan Glynn and Karen Gulliver, whose scrupulous pens were vital in helping me render a more fluent and accessible story. I owe as well a special thank you to Bold Story Press, Emily Barrosse, Julianna Scott Fein, and the team, for believing in *This Arab Life* and for their unwavering support.

When I shared the first draft with those who have known me longest and best, the general consensus was to run with the book but to lighten up on the heartbreak. Every drenched day has its rainbows, after all, so in subsequent iterations I have tried not to lose sight of the rays. But inevitably, I had to be faithful to the temperament of the age and my sense of it. I also had to be true to the tortured past that gave shape to this age. The anguish, therefore, remains obstinately present, sharing space with the personal memories that are tellingly sweeter and lighter. These juxtapositions, sharp and jarring, illuminate the many chasms that fill *This Arab Life*.

Notes

Chapter 1

1 Sebastian Haffner, *Defying Hitler: A Memoir* (London: Weidenfeld & Nicolson, 2012), 81.

2 Joel Beinin & Frédéric Vairel, *Social Movements, Mobilization, and Contestation in the Middle East and North Africa* (Stanford: Stanford University Press, 2013), 1.

3 Pankaj Mishra, *Age of Anger* (New York: Farrar, Straus and Giroux, 2017), 158.

Chapter 2

1 Abd al-Rahman Munif, *Story of a City* (London: Quartet, 1996), v.

Chapter 3

1 Hazem Kandil, *The Power Triangle, Military, Security and Politics in Regime Change* (New York: Oxford University Press, 2016), 87.

2 Ibid, 71–75.

3 Munif, *Story of a City*, 104.

Chapter 4

1 Arwa Salih, *The Stillborn: Notes of a Woman from the Student Movement Generation in Egypt* (New York: Seagull Books, 2018), 16, 18.

2 Wael Sawah, "Baynama Kunna Na'shaq wa Nughanni, Kanat Akhawatuna Yatahajabn" [When We Were Falling In Love and Singing, Our Sisters Were Veiling]. *Daraj*, October 12, 2018. Author's translation.

3 Joel Beinin, *Civil Society, Social Movements, and the Arab Uprisings of 2011* (Stanford University Press, August 2013), 13.

4 Guilain Denoeux and Dima Toukan, *Civil Society Assessment.* Produced for the United States Agency for International Development, with contribution from Hanna Theodorie and Patricia Hunter (USAID, 2016), 7.

5 Ahmad Awad and Rania Sarayra, *Enabling Environment National Assessment. Country Report: Jordan* (Amman: Phoenix Center for Economic and Informatics Studies, 2015), 6.

6 Guilain Denoeux and Dima Toukan, *Civil Society Investment Report* (USAID/Jordan Monitoring & Evaluation Support Project, 2016), 7.

7 Arwa Salih, *The Stillborn,* 33.

Chapter 5

1 Fawwaz Traboulsi, *Janoub al-Yaman Fi Hukm al-Yassar: Shahadat Shakhsieyah* [Southern Yemen Under the Rule of the Left: A Personal Testimony] (Beirut: Riad al-Rayyes Press, 2015), 86. Author's translation.

2 Mishra, *Age of Anger,* 136.

3 Safia Saadeh, "Uridu Abi" [I Want My Father Back], *An-Nahar Literary Supplement,* July 4, 1992.

4 Aron Lund, "The Miserable Afterlife of Michel Aflaq," *Diwan* (blog), *Carnegie Middle East Center,* March 10, 2014, https://carnegie-mec. org/diwan/54844.

5 Ibid.

Chapter 6

1 "War by Other Means, Syria's Economic Struggle," *Synaps,* September 30, 2019.

2 Eva Bellin, "The Robustness of Authoritarianism in the Middle East: Exceptionalism in Comparative Perspective." *Comparative Politics,* no. 2 (January 2004):139–157.

3 Philippe Fargues, "Mass Migration and Uprisings in Arab Countries: An Analytical Framework" in G. Luciani (ed.) *Combining Economic and Political Development: The Experience of MENA,* International Development Policy, series 7 (Geneva: Graduate Institute Publications, Boston: Brill-Nijhoff, 2017), 175. The states included in this calculation are Lebanon, Syria, Jordan, Palestine, Morocco, Algeria, Tunisia, and Egypt.

4 Asef Bayat, *Revolutions Without Revolutionaries: Making Sense of the Arab Spring,* (Stanford: Stanford University Press, 2017), 17.

5 Ibid, 11.

6 Frédéric Vairel, *Authoritarianisms and Oppositions in Social Movements, Mobilization, and Contestation in the Middle East and North Africa* (Stanford: Stanford University Press, 2013), 34.

7 Joel Beinin, "The Rise of Egypt's Workers," *The Carnegie Papers, Middle East* (June 2012): 3–5.

8 Beinin, *Civil Society*, 40.
9 Arezki Metref, "Algeria's Massive Movement for Change," *Le Monde Diplomatique*, December 2019, http://www.mondiplo.com.

Chapter 7

1 Fawwaz Traboulsi, *The History of Modern Lebanon* (London: Pluto Press, 2012), 181.
2 Samir Kassir, *Tareekh Bayrout* [The History of Beirut] (Beirut: Dar An-Nahar Publishing, 2003), 22 & 25. Author's translation.
3 Dominique Eddé, "The Compatibility of Opposites: A Portrait of Lebanon," *The New York Review of Books*, June 19, 2019, https://www.nybooks.com.
4 Ibid.
5 Mohammad Zbeib, "Massader al Azma: Takreess Nizam al Harb" [The Origins of the Crisis: The Consecration of the War's System], *Al Akhbar Newspaper* (Beirut), October 8, 2018.
6 Fouad Ajami, *The Vanished Imam* (Ithaca: Cornell University Press, 1987), 21.

Chapter 9

1 Vivian Yee, "Desperate to Leave Beirut, Young Lebanese Are Also the Ones Fixing It," *New York Times*, August 27, 2020.

References

Ajami, Fouad. *The Vanished Imam*. Ithaca: Cornell University Press, 1987.

Awad, Ahmad, and Rania Sarayra. *Enabling Environment National Assessment. Country Report: Jordan*. Amman: Phoenix Center for Economic and Informatics Studies, 2015.

Bayat, Asef. *Revolutions Without Revolutionaries: Making Sense of the Arab Spring*. Stanford: Stanford University Press, 2017.

Beinin, Joel. "The Rise of Egypt's Workers." *The Carnegie Papers, Middle East*, June 2012.

Beinin, Joel. *Civil Society, Social Movements, and the Arab Uprisings of 2011*. Stanford: Stanford University Press, 2013.

Beinin, Joel, and Frédéric Vairel, ed. *Social Movements, Mobilization, and Contestation in the Middle East and North Africa*. Stanford: Stanford University Press, 2013.

Bellin, Eva. "The Robustness of Authoritarianism in the Middle East: Exceptionalism in Comparative Perspective." *Comparative Politics* 36, no. 2 (January 2004): 139–157.

Denoeux, Guilain, and Dima Toukan. *Civil Society Assessment, produced for the United States Agency for International Development*. With contribution from Hanna Theodorie and Patricia Hunter. *USAID*, 2016.

Denoeux, Guilain, and Dima Toukan. *Civil Society Investment Report*. USAID/Jordan Monitoring & Evaluation Support Project, 2016.

Eddé, Dominique. "The Compatibility of Opposites: A Portrait of Lebanon." *The New York Review of Books.* June 19, 2019. https://www.nybooks.com/daily/2019/06/19/the-compatibility-of-opposites-a-portrait-of-lebanon/.

Fargues, Philippe. "Mass Migration and Uprisings in Arab Countries: An Analytical Framework" in G. Luciani (ed.) *Combining Economic and Political Development: The Experience of MENA,* International Development Policy, series 7 (Geneva: Graduate Institute Publications, Boston: Brill-Nijhoff), 2017.

Haffner, Sebastian. *Defying Hitler: A Memoir.* London: Weidenfeld & Nicolson, 2012.

Kandil, Hazem. *The Power Triangle, Military, Security and Politics in Regime Change.* New York: Oxford University Press, 2016.

Kassir, Samir. *Tareekh Bayrout* [The History of Beirut]. Beirut: Dar An-Nahar Publishing, 2003.

Lund, Aron. "The Miserable Afterlife of Michel Aflaq." *Diwan* (blog). *Carnegie Middle East Center,* March 10, 2014. https://carnegie-mec.org/diwan/54844.

Metref, Arezki. "Algeria's Massive Movement for Change." *Le Monde Diplomatique,* December 2019. http://www.mondiplo.com.

Mishra, Pankaj. *Age of Anger.* New York: Farrar, Straus and Giroux, 2017.

Munif, Abd al-Rahman. *Story of a City.* London: Quartet, 1996.

Saadeh, Safia. "Uridu Abi" [I Want My Father Back]. *An-Nahar Literary Supplement,* July 4, 1992.

Salih, Arwa. *The Stillborn: Notes of a Woman from the Student Movement Generation in Egypt.* New York: Seagull Books, 2018.

Sawah, Wael. "Baynama Kunna Na'shaq wa Nughanni, Kanat Akhawatuna Yatahajabn" [When We Were Falling In Love and Singing, Our sisters Were Veiling]. *Daraj,* October 12, 2018. http://www.Daraj.com.

Synaps Syria Team. "War by Other Means, Syria's Economic Struggle." *Synaps,* September 30, 2019. https://www.synaps.network/post/syria-conflict-economy-corruption-sanctions.

Traboulsi, Fawwaz, *The History of Modern Lebanon.* 2nd ed. London: Pluto Press, 2012.

Traboulsi, Fawwaz. *Janoub al-Yaman Fi Hukm al-Yassar: Shahadat Shakhsieyah* [Southern Yemen Under the Rule of the Left: A Personal Testimony]. Beirut: Riad al-Rayyes Press, 2015.

Vairel, Frédéric. *Authoritarianisms and Oppositions in Social Movements, Mobilization, and Contestation in the Middle East and North Africa.* Stanford: Stanford University Press, 2013.

Yee, Vivian. "Desperate to Leave Beirut, Young Lebanese Are Also the Ones Fixing It." *New York Times,* August 27, 2020. https://www.nytimes.com/2020/08/27/world/middleeast/beirut-explosion-volunteers.html.

Zbeib, Mohammad. "Massader al-Azmah: Takreess Nizam al-Harb" [The Origins of the Crisis: The Consecration of the War's System]. *Al Akhbar* (Beirut), October 8, 2018. https://www.al-akhbar.com.

Bold Story Press is a curated, woman-owned hybrid publishing company with a mission of publishing well-written stories by women. If your book is chosen for publication, our team of expert editors and designers will work with you to publish a professionally edited and designed book. Every woman has a story to tell. If you have written yours and want to explore publishing with Bold Story Press, contact us at https://boldstorypress.com.

BOLD STORY PRESS

The Bold Story Press logo, designed by Grace Arsenault, was inspired by the nom de plume, or pen name, a sad necessity at one time for female authors who wanted to publish. The woman's face hidden in the quill is the profile of Virginia Woolf, who, in addition to being an early feminist writer, founded and ran her own publishing company, Hogarth Press.

Printed in Great Britain
by Amazon

23639365R00098